Spectacular Plants

& how to grOW them

RHS

Wild Nature Press Ltd
Registered address
7 Sandy Court,
Ashleigh Way,
Plymouth, PL7 5JX.

www.wildnaturepress.com

Published in 2019

Copyright text © Stewart McPherson 2019
Copyright photographs and illustrations © as credited on page 158

The right of Stewart McPherson to be identified as the author of this work has been asserted by him in accordance with the Copyright, Designs and Patents Act 1988.

All rights reserved. No part of this publication may be reproduced or used in any form or by any means – photographic, electronic or mechanical, including photocopying, recording, taping or information storage or retrieval systems – without permission of the publishers.

A CIP catalogue record for this book is available from the British Library

ISBN 978-1-9995811-2-1

Printed in Slovenia on behalf of Latitude Press Limited

10 9 8 7 6 5 4 3 2 1

To Louis and Jasmine,
I hope that you may fall in love with these
spectacular plants as much as I did during my childhood

The Don Hanson Charitable Foundation sponsored the donation of one copy of this book to be sent to each of 10,000 primary schools across the UK. Royalties from the sale of this book supports the Don Hanson Charitable Foundation's on-going work to inspire children's interests in learning about nature, science and the conservation of our world.

RHS

Spectacular Plants & how to grow them

Stewart McPherson

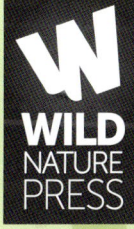

WILD NATURE PRESS

Contents

Spectacular plants — 6
- What is a plant? — 7
  - Photosynthesis — 8
- Types of plants — 9
  - How do plants with seeds reproduce? — 10
  - How do plants without seeds reproduce? — 11
  - The world's most spectacular plants — 12
  - Where are the most spectacular plants found? — 13
- World map of common habitats — 14
- Common habitats — 16

Golden rules — 18

Carnivorous plants — 20
- What is a carnivorous plant? — 21
- Where do carnivorous plants come from? — 22
- Types of carnivorous plant — 22
- Sundews — 24
- Butterworts — 26
- Bladderworts — 28
- Tropical pitcher plants — 30
- North American pitcher plants — 32
- Marsh pitcher plants — 34
- Albany Pitcher Plant — 36
- Venus' Flytrap — 38

Unbelievable flowers — 46
- Largest single flower — 48
- Largest branched flower scape — 49
- Largest unbranched flower scape — 50
- Queen of the Andes — 52
- Faces in the flowers — 54
- Scary flowers — 58
- Hot Lips Flower — 60
- Four O'Clock Flower — 61
- Bat flowers — 62
- Bird of paradise flower — 63
- Lobster claw flowers — 64
- Passion flowers — 66
- The colours of flowers — 68

World's smelliest flowers — 70
- Why do some flowers stink? — 71
- Where do the smelliest flowers and fruit come from? — 72
  - Smelly Feet Tree — 72
- Parasitic flowers — 73
- Deadly deceptor plants — 74
- Stinky 'King of Fruit' — 75
- Starfish flowers — 76
- Arums — 82
  - Dragon Lily — 83
- Giant arums — 86
- Voodoo Lily — 92

Funky fruit & veg — 94

- Rainbow carrots — 96
- White strawberries — 98
- Black tomatoes — 100
- Purple potatoes — 102
- Jewel corn — 106
- Cucamelons — 110
- Super-shaped watermelons — 112
- Dragon fruit — 116

Sensitive plants — 120

- Where do sensitive plants come from? — 121
- Why do sensitive plants move? — 121
- Exploding seed pods! — 122
  - Wood sorrels — 122
  - Squirting Cucumber — 123
- Sensitive Mimosa — 124
- Little Tree Plant — 126
- Dancing Plant — 128

Unbelievable spectacular plants — 132

- Iridescent-leaved plants — 133
- Darth Vader Begonia — 135
- Amazing airplants — 136
- Beautiful bromeliads — 138
- Spectacular succulents — 140
- Cool cacti — 143
- Armoured plants — 146
- Greenhouse plants — 147
- Record holders — 148
  - The biggest seed — 148
  - The biggest leaf — 149
  - The tallest tree — 149
  - The most massive tree — 150
  - Oldest plant on earth — 151
  - Other time travellers — 152
- Amazing bonsais — 154

Sourcing spectacular plants — 156

How to grow index — 160

Spectacular Plants

We are surrounded by plants. Whether you live in the countryside or in a city, on the edge of a rainforest or a desert, plants are everywhere. They provide food, medicines, clothing, building materials and fuel, not to mention regulating our weather and providing shelter to the majority of land animals worldwide. Plants really are vital to our survival.

There are approximately 400,000 plant species currently known to science, with about 2,000 new species described by botanists (plant scientists) every year! About 94% of plants are flowering plants (from grasses and daises to giant flowering rainforest trees) while the other 6% are non-flowering plants (which include cone-bearing trees such as pines).

Of the known plant species, about 21% are threatened with extinction, mainly because of habitat loss due to human activities and the current, higher than usual rate of climate change. However, many people around the world are working hard to make sure that these at-risk species don't disappear forever.

WHAT IS A PLANT?

We all know what 'plants' are, but describing what a plant is can really challenge people! Not all plants have leaves, and not all plants have flowers, so we have to be really specific. All plants fall into the biological kingdom called Plantae and, while they are some of the most varied of all living organisms on the planet, most plants have the following characteristics:

- They are made up of lots of cells that together form different parts of the plant
- Most of them make their own food in their green leaves, using sunlight (photosynthesis)

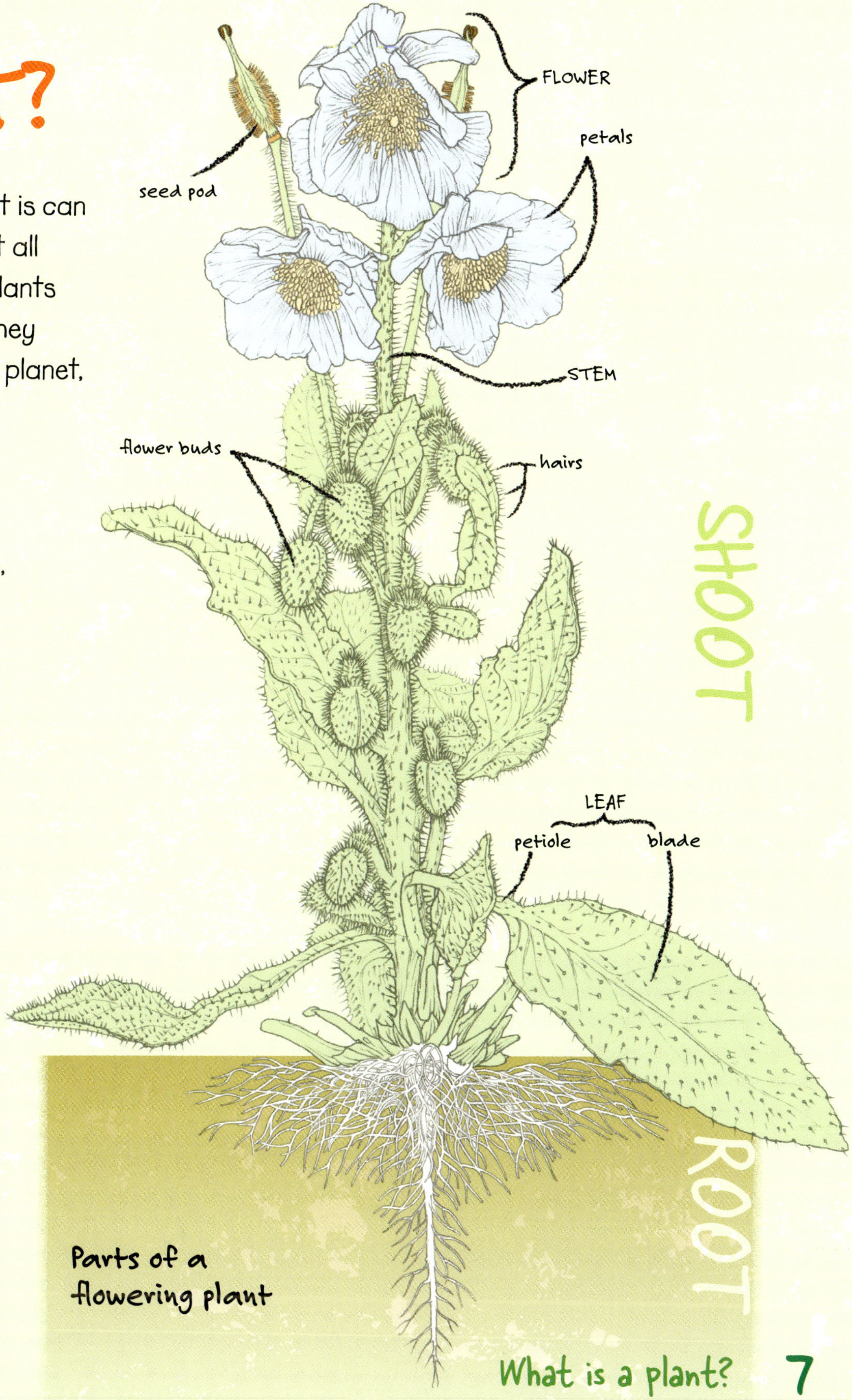

Parts of a flowering plant

PHOTOSYNTHESIS

Photosynthesis is the process that plants use to make their own food. The waste product of this is oxygen. Did you know that until plants and green algae grew in the oceans and on the land, pumping out oxygen into the air, there was not enough oxygen in the atmosphere for animals to live!

This is exactly why plants are so important to us. Not only do they provide most of the food that we eat, they literally provide the oxygen that we need to stay alive, and store away the greenhouse gas carbon dioxide, helping to regulate our climate.

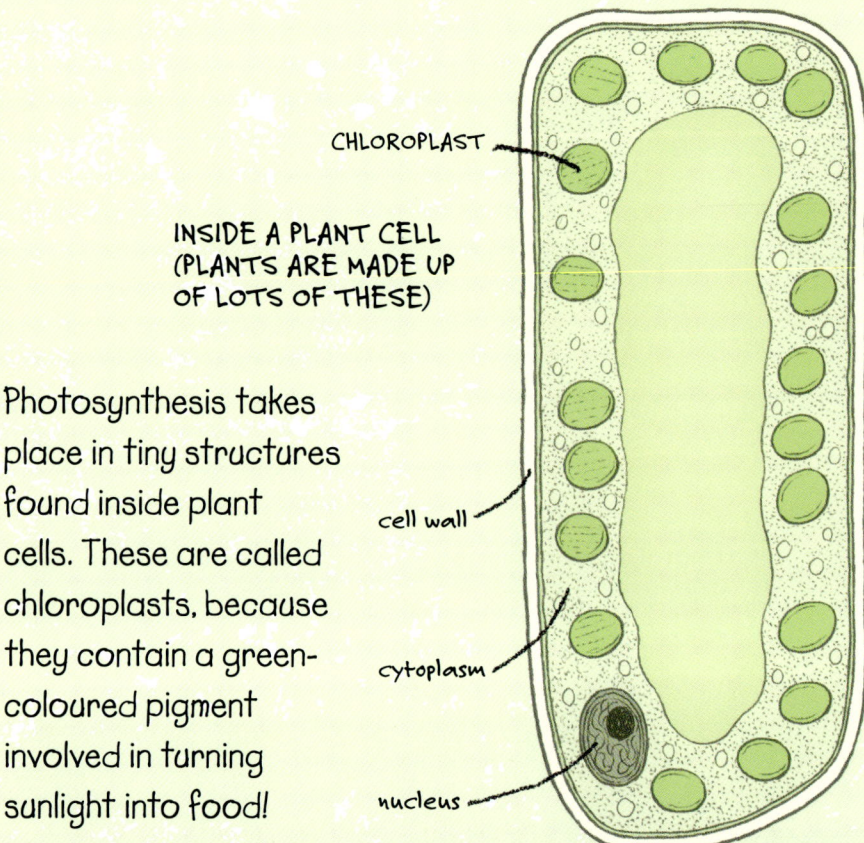

INSIDE A PLANT CELL (PLANTS ARE MADE UP OF LOTS OF THESE)

Photosynthesis takes place in tiny structures found inside plant cells. These are called chloroplasts, because they contain a green-coloured pigment involved in turning sunlight into food!

THERE'S ALWAYS ONE...

...exception to the rule, that is! In fact, hundreds of plants don't photosynthesise. Some live underground off dead and decaying material, some (like mistletoe, pictured right) live as parasites on the branches of other plants, tapping into their hosts to steal sugars and minerals, while some plants, like the giant-flowered Rafflesia, live inside other plants and only show themselves when they need to reproduce. All of these plants had ancestors that used to photosynthesise – evolution has just taken them in weird and wonderful directions!

8   Spectacular plants

TYPES OF PLANTS

The plant kingdom is divided up into numerous smaller groups.

MOSSES, LIVERWORTS & HORNWORTS (Bryophytes)

These plants don't have the water and food transporting pipes found in stems, so they are limited in size and grow low to the ground. They are mainly found in permanently damp habitats. They do not make seeds, instead they make spores to reproduce. There are about 20,000 species worldwide.

SEED BEARING PLANTS (Spermatophytes)

These plants have stems with transportation pipes that mean they can grow tall and large, they produce seeds to reproduce. They can be sorted into further groups and include many of the plants you might recognise on a day to day basis.

CONE-BEARING PLANTS (Gymnosperms)

Including pine trees, cedars, cypresses, firs and cycads, amongst others.

FLOWERING PLANTS (Angiosperms)

Worldwide there are at least 370,000 species of flowering plants – the largest group of plants on Earth!

FERNS, HORSETAILS & CLUBMOSSES (Pteridophytes)

These plants grow with tall stems that have pipes to transport water and food. They are similar to mosses as they make spores to reproduce. Worldwide there are about 11,800 species.

Types of plants 9

How do plants with seeds reproduce?

Since most plants on Earth are flowering plants (angiosperms), plant reproduction usually involves flowers.

Flowers are the reproductive parts of plants and they usually (though not always) have male and female parts.

The male parts produce pollen which must be transferred to the female parts. The movement of pollen is called pollination and this can be carried out by insects like bees, wasps, beetles and butterflies, by the wind or even raindrops. In some plants, pollination can happen automatically inside an unopened flower! Seeds will be formed in the ovary and each seed could grow into a whole new plant.

Flowers come in so many amazing arrays of colour and form precisely because they often have to compete with each other for pollinators. Some plants, like bee orchids, take this to the extreme, by mimicking female insects to entice males to mate with them.

A few seed-bearing plants however do not produce flowers or fruit, for example conifers, these are called gymnosperms (meaning 'naked seed'). They produce millions of pollen grains which are only dispersed by the wind to enable pollination. Gymnosperms first appeared about 285 million years ago, about 150 million years before flowering plants evolved, and about 1,000 species are alive worldwide today!

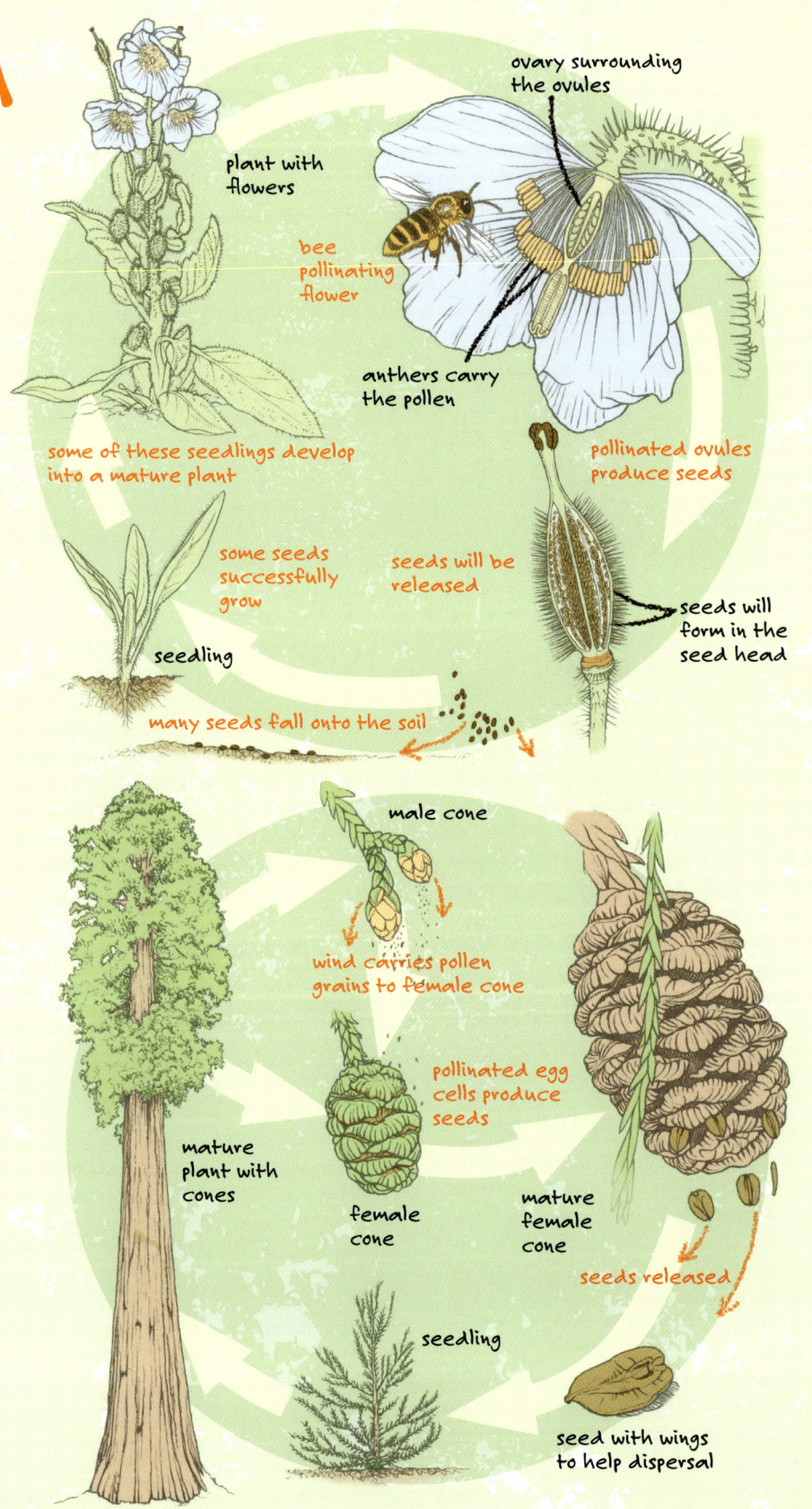

10 Spectacular plants

How do plants without seeds reproduce?

Spores are single-celled structures used by members of the moss and fern families to create new plants. In ferns they are produced by spore capsules that grow on the back of the leaves. The spore capsules look like tiny, fluffy, orange beads.

When the spores are fully mature, they are released from the spore capsule into the environment. Once they land in a moist and protected spot, they start to grow and develop into little plants. These may be flat and look more like liverworts or moss-like growths. They will then get bigger over time and eventually grow into ferns.

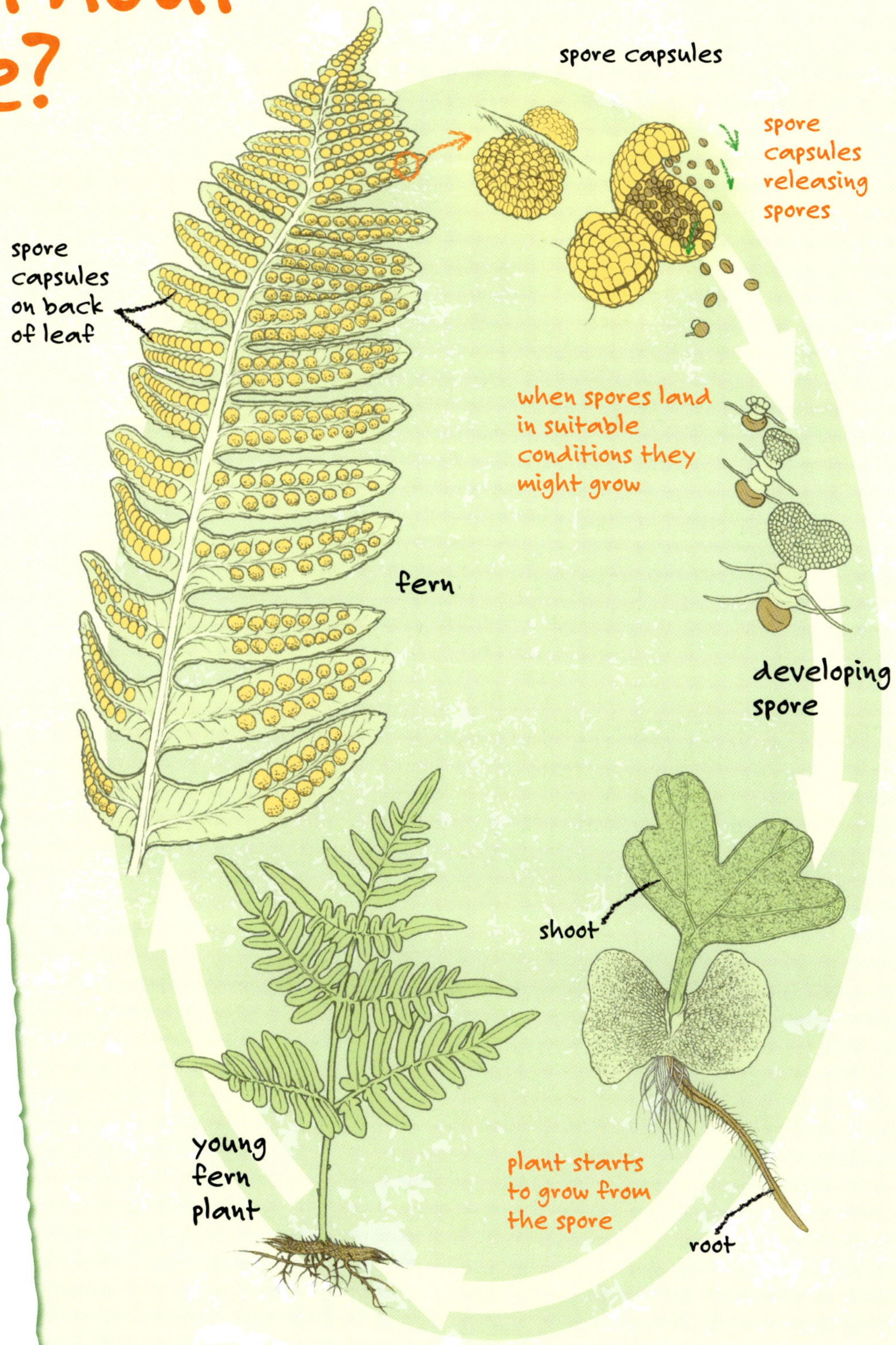

Many plants are capable of asexual reproduction. A good example of this is when gardeners take leaf or stem cuttings to produce new plants. This is the process of making a clone of the parent plant. The pieces they cut off and plant in the soil will eventually grow to become little plants of their own!

spore capsules

spore capsules releasing spores

spore capsules on back of leaf

when spores land in suitable conditions they might grow

fern

developing spore

shoot

young fern plant

plant starts to grow from the spore

root

How do plants reproduce? 11

The world's most spectacular plants

With so many different species found across almost every habitat on Earth, it shouldn't be a surprise to learn that plants are incredibly varied. The result of this diversity is that there are huge numbers of really weird and wonderful plants that most of us have never heard of. There are some truly amazing, standout plants among them, including plants that eat insects, plants with leaves that shine like dazzling blue metals, plants with single flowers a metre across, plants that smell worse than rotten garbage – including at least one that many people love to eat – food plants that come in odd colours and shapes, plants whose flowers look like animals or body parts, and plants that move, or even dance (if slowly)!

This book will introduce you to just a fraction of the spectacular plants that are known to us and, with luck, may set you on a path to discovering hundreds more species as you develop your own interests in your favourite plant groups. Some of these strange and wonderful plants are just too specialised for most people, or even botanic gardens, to grow in captivity. Perhaps you may be lucky enough to discover them in the wild some day! However, there are dozens more that you can grow to add interest to your own home or garden, or a little weirdness to your dining table. These plants will open a door to endless possibilities and a lifetime of new discoveries!

Where are the world's most spectacular plants found?

It may surprise you to learn that some of the world's most spectacular plants may come from the countryside around us. Whether or not you've ever encountered one is another matter, since many plants will only grow in one type of habitat, and this may not be where you live. However, with a little research, it can be rewarding to successfully locate and photograph native species – like a treasure hunt for nature. And for species that cannot be found in your stomping ground, botanic gardens and specialist nurseries are the best places to try and see them.

Spectacular plants come from all sorts of habitats around the world, from the driest deserts, which typically give rise to drought-tolerant succulent plants, to hot and humid rainforests, where luxurious foliage and flamboyant flowers are most common.

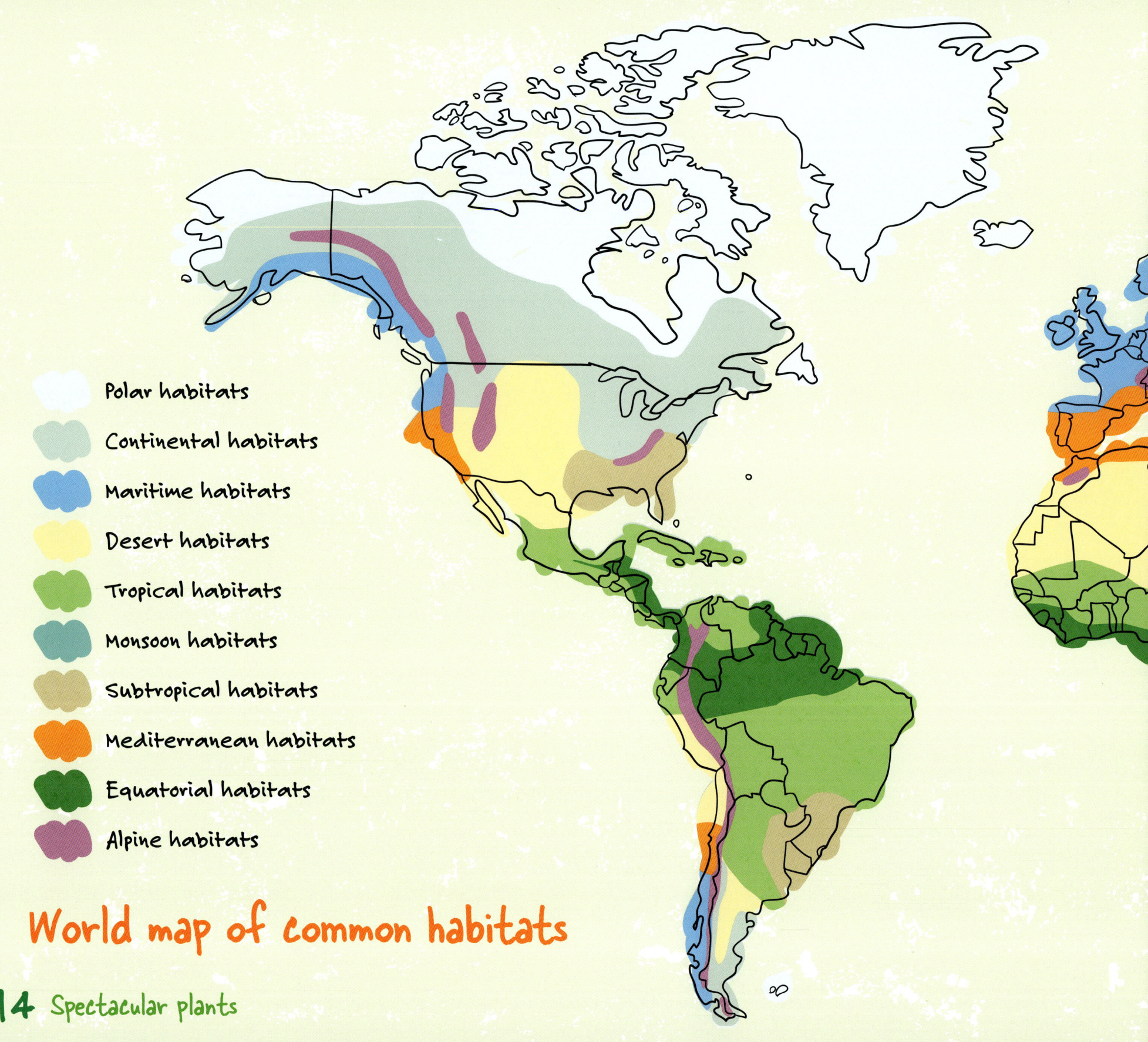

World map of common habitats

14 Spectacular plants

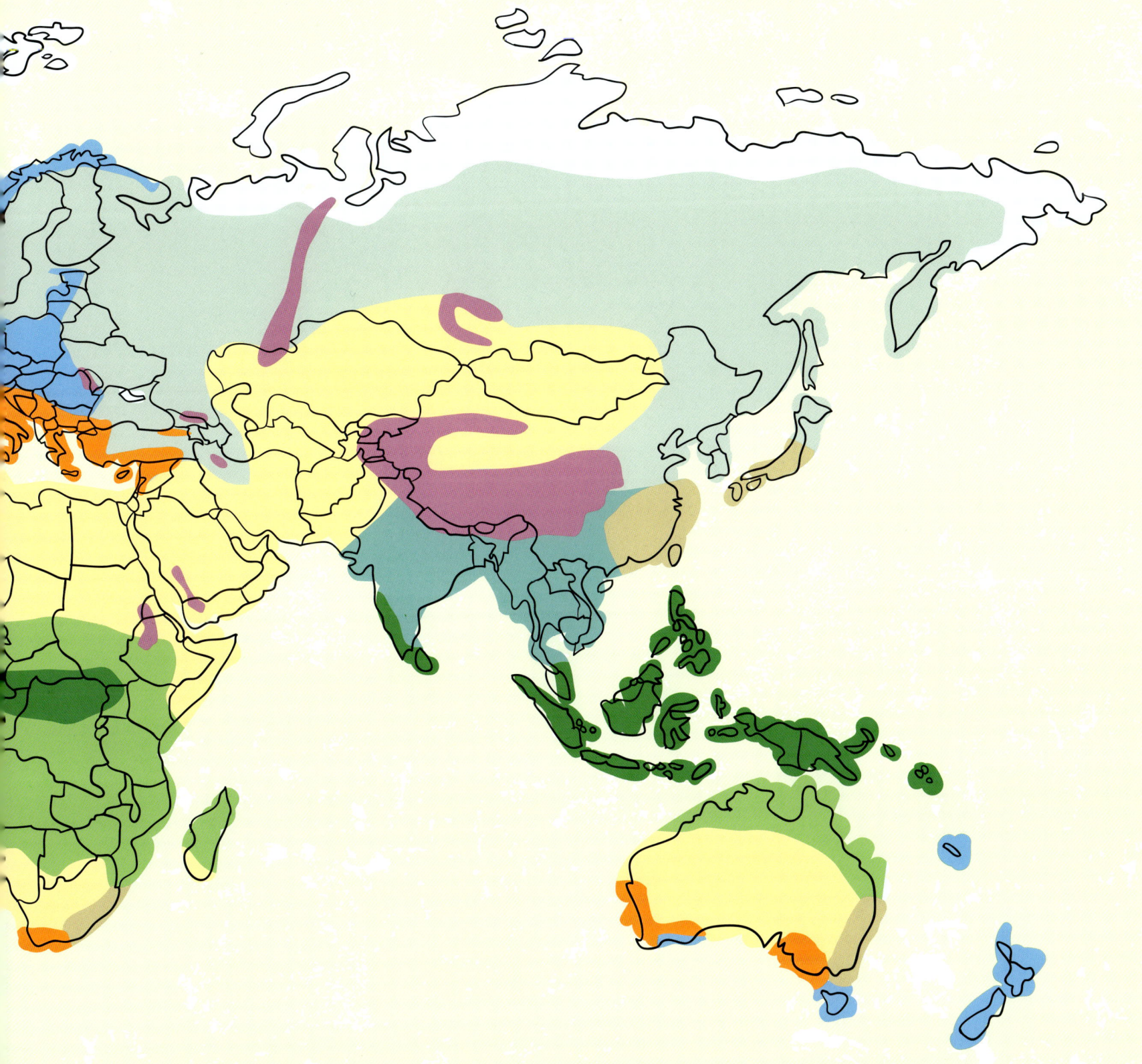

World map of common habitats 15

Some of the most common habitats worldwide are:

TROPICAL

Tropical habitats are found close to the equator and are generally warm (more than 18°C) throughout the year. They are generally wet, or have wet and dry seasons, though in some places the 'dry season' isn't that dry, just less wet! They are the most diverse habitats of all and are rich with plant and animal life, which flourish with the year-round warmth and moisture.

MEDITERRANEAN

Though named after the climate found around the Mediterranean Sea, these habitats are also found in other places around the world. They usually have rainy winters and dry summers – the summers may be warm to hot, while the winters range from cool to cold, with a low likelihood of prolonged frosty weather. With few weather extremes, biodiversity is high, with some diversity hotspots found in places like South Africa and the south-west of Western Australia.

SUBTROPICAL

These habitats are found either side of the equator, just north and south of the tropics. They usually have warm to hot summers and mild winters. Rainfall tends to be concentrated in summer months, with cool, drier winters. Species diversity is generally high in the subtropics.

MARITIME

These habitats usually have cool summers and winters, without a large swing in temperature between summer and winter. This approximately translates, more or less, to summers in the mid-20s celsius, and winters close to freezing. These habitats are sometimes called oceanic because of their proximity to warm seas and oceans preventing large temperature changes.

16 Spectacular plants

CONTINENTAL

Continental habitats are less affected by the world's seas, and experience large swings in temperature. Summers are warm to hot, and often humid, while winters may be below 0°C for several months each winter. The number of species is lower, but many of them have special adaptations to survive the strong seasonal changes.

ALPINE

Alpine habitats are typical of high mountain ranges and plateaus, the most significant in the world being the mighty Himalayas. In these habitats, the average temperature throughout the year is less than 10°C, being of course much colder in winter. Diversity is low owing to the limited growing season and harsh conditions, but plants may be highly specialised to survive cold and drought.

DESERT

There are regions where annual rainfall is too low to support significant vegetation cover. Plants from these areas are usually adapted to survive for months or years without rain, or to absorb water from seasonal rains, or even mists and fog! Highest diversity occurs in areas closest to the subtropics, where seasonal rainfall is slightly higher.

POLAR

In the far north of both Asia and North America the summers are so short and cold that only low-growing, tough vegetation can survive. This mostly treeless landscape is called tundra. Shrubs, grasses and mosses are the most common plants, while the few trees that occur are compact and slow-growing, almost like natural bonsai. At the very extreme limits, such as Greenland and Antarctica, a permanent layer of ice may cover the ground, preventing any plants from growing at all!

Common habitats

Golden rules

When it comes to collecting and growing plants, there are a number of golden rules that you should bear in mind. They don't just concern how you grow your plants, but also how you choose them. Observing these rules will help to ensure your success when growing different kinds of plants with different requirements.

LOCATION, LOCATION, LOCATION!

Identify the best places in your home and garden for growing plants. Different spots will vary in terms of the amount of light, humidity and, of course, temperature that they offer. This will help you to choose the plants best suited to your conditions.

BE REALISTIC

Choose the right plant for the right space. Sometimes we encounter plants that we really want to grow, even though we can't offer them the conditions that they need. Keeping an outdoor plant indoors in the warm over winter, or keeping a tropical plant in cold, dark conditions will usually fail and leave you disappointed. If you can't offer the right conditions, you might be able to create a suitable space. Temperature controlled greenhouses, conservatories and aquariums mounted with lights are examples, but will require time and money to set up.

DEVELOP GOOD GROWING HABITS

Providing the right conditions is especially important in the case of water. While many plants are happy kept slightly damp at all times, others like their soil to dry out for a while before receiving more water. Overwatering is one of the biggest killers, but a good quality, well-draining soil will help you to avoid such losses. Dry air caused by central heating systems can also stress plants out, leading to browning of leaves and poor growth. By growing them in groups, or occasionally misting them to increase humidity, you will make your plants much happier.

A GOOD REST

Many plants slow down their growth in winter. When this happens, they should be watered and fertilised less often and kept at slightly cooler conditions. When spring arrives, a good winter rest beforehand will ensure vigorous new growth and possibly flowers, too.

KEEP AN EYE OUT FOR PESTS

Occasionally, pest insects may appear on your plants. These may be just a few in number, in which case they can be removed by hand using a soft tissue dipped in soapy water. If left unchecked, however, a small pest problem can turn into an infestation. Pests commonly arrive on new plants, so it is good practice to keep new plants in quarantine for a few days – place them in a spot by themselves until you are sure that they aren't carrying any nasty beasties.

THAT TASTES... POISONOUS!

As a general rule, don't eat your plants unless you know that they are regarded as safe fruits or vegetables – many innocent looking houseplants can make you ill if eaten!

BE PATIENT

Plants can be purchased as seeds, seedlings or adults. There are different reasons for buying one form or another – adults generally cost more, but they are fully developed and you can see exactly how they look, although they are likely to get bigger. Seeds and seedlings are much cheaper, but you will have to raise them into adulthood before they flower, which can take months. However, sowing seeds allows you to watch their development from seed to flowering adult, which gives you a great feeling of achievement.

RESPONSIBLE PURCHASING

It is important to buy your plants and seeds from trusted sources for a couple of reasons. You can be sure that plants sold by good nurseries and specialists will be healthy and correctly labelled. Their plants and seeds are also less likely to be illegally taken from the wild. When purchasing online, especially from websites like eBay, you must be careful of sellers offering seeds of incredible-looking plants like 'rainbow coloured roses' or 'blue Venus' Flytraps' – these plants simply don't exist, and the seeds are usually repackaged seeds of cheap garden herbs. If the item being sold looks too good to be true, it is usually a fake! While it is good to check the reviews of sellers stocking these items for negative feedback, remember that recipients have a limited time to review purchases – by the time their seeds have grown large enough for them to realise that something is wrong, they cannot change their reviews.

Carnivorous Plants

Did you know that there are plants that can catch, kill and digest animals? Well there are, and the Venus' Flytrap isn't the only one! Not only that, the largest of them all are big enough to trap small mammals like rats and shrews, not to mention small birds. These killers have managed to turn the tables on animals, making plants the hunter rather than the hunted. They are therefore some of the most unusual and highly specialised of all plants in the world.

WHAT is a carnivorous plant?

To be carnivorous, a plant must:

1. Attract prey
2. Trap prey
3. Digest prey (some species rely on bacteria and fungi for this)
4. Absorb nutrients from prey.

By doing this, carnivorous plants can obtain everything that they need to grow – except for energy, which they produce from sunlight like other plants.

Sticky sundew droplets attract and trap insects like this fly

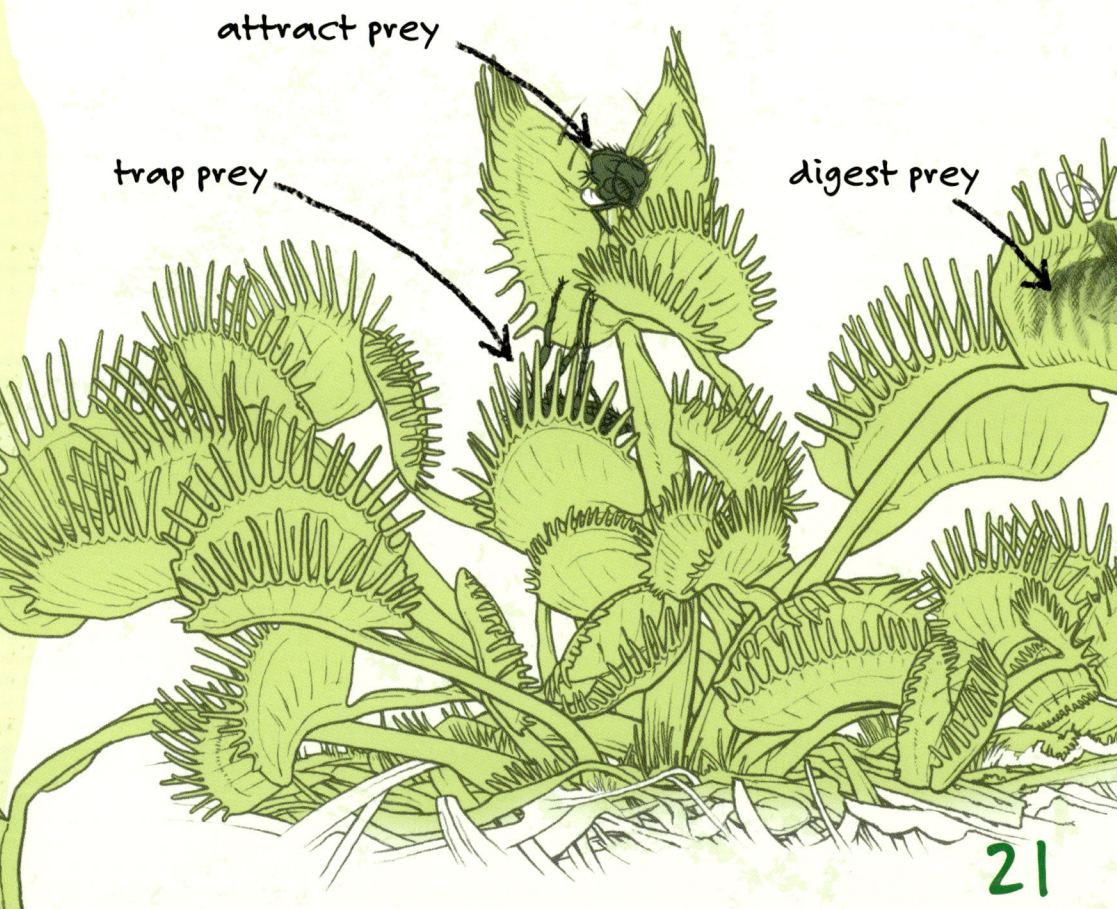

attract prey

trap prey

digest prey

WHY do carnivorous plants even exist?

Like animals, plants need a number of things in order to survive, chief among them being a source of nutrients to help them to grow. While animals eat other animals or plants to gain nutrients, plants usually absorb nutrients from the soil. Some soils, like those in swamps, are very poor in nutrients and so the plants that live on them have to develop ways to survive. One of these ways is carnivory – the eating of animal tissue.

Where do carnivorous plants come from?

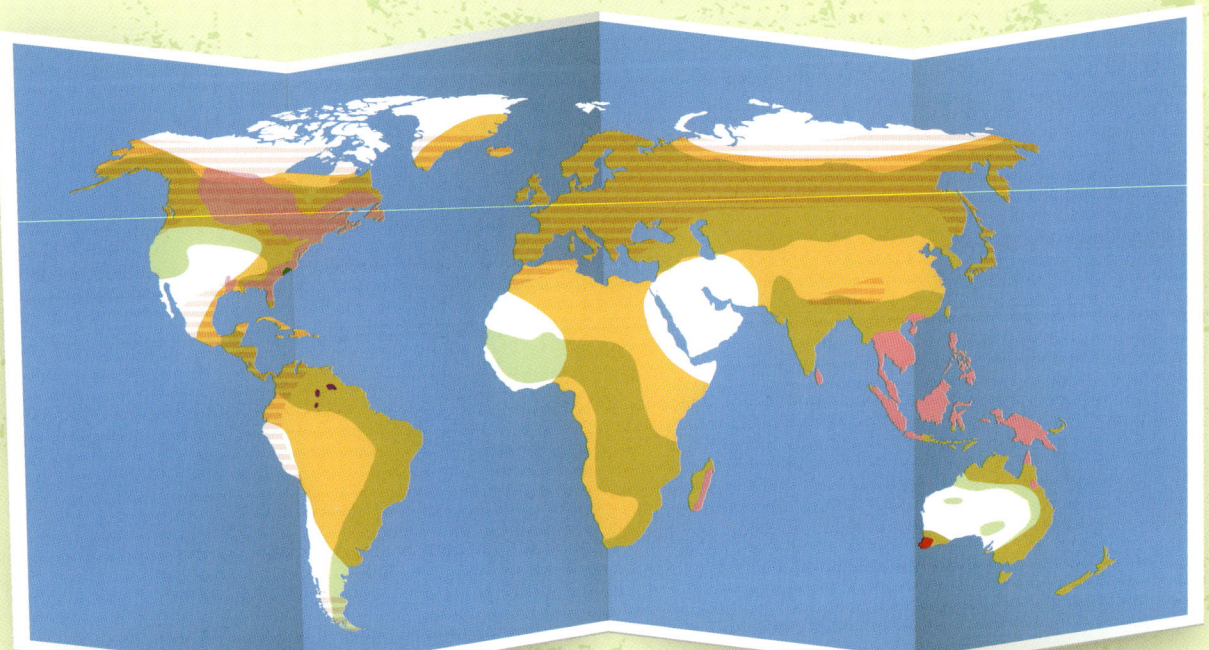

Carnivorous plants occur on every continent except Antarctica! Most species can be found in tropical and subtropical areas – especially South America, Africa and Australia – but 13 species are found in the UK, and about 70 species in North America.

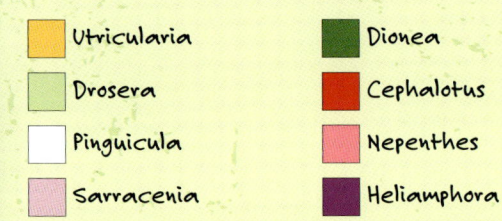

- Utricularia
- Drosera
- Pinguicula
- Sarracenia
- Dionea
- Cephalotus
- Nepenthes
- Heliamphora

TYPES OF CARNIVOROUS PLANT

There are nearly 700 species of carnivorous plants which are split into five main groups based on how they trap their prey. Flypaper traps are by far the most common of all carnivorous plants, with more than 300 known species. One group of flypaper traps, the sundews (*Drosera*), has more species than any other carnivorous plant group.

These groups, listed here from most to least common, are:

Flypaper traps

These are sticky-leaved traps that grab hold of insects with a sort of glue. The insects are digested by enzymes directly on the leaves of the plant.

Bladder traps

These are highly specialised underwater traps shaped like little bags. They suck in prey like a vacuum as they swim past and digest them within, just like animal stomachs!

22 Carnivorous plants

Pitfall traps

These traps are shaped like pitchers and contain pools of digestive enzymes. With slippery walls coated with wax, any animals that fall into them are unable to escape. They include the largest of all carnivorous plants.

Lobster-pot traps

These traps are similar to the lobster and crab traps used by fishermen. Once a prey animal wanders in, they rarely manage to find their way out!

Snap traps

The most famous of all carnivorous plants — the Venus' Flytrap — is a snap trap. It has leaves that clamp shut when prey wander in, holding them tight and digesting them within!

THE LARGEST CARNIVOROUS PLANT OF ALL!

The largest carnivorous plants are the tropical pitcher plants, known as *Nepenthes*. The biggest of these is the King Pitcher Plant (*Nepenthes rajah*), which has traps up to 40cm long, capable of holding 3.5 litres of water. It is known to trap rodents!

Nepenthes rajah

Carnivorous plants 23

SUNDEWS (Drosera)

Sundews are amazing carnivorous plants with leaves covered in glistening droplets of sticky glue that looks just like harmless dew. Insects unfortunate enough to land on the leaves of a sundew are immediately held fast by this glue. They become even more covered as they struggle, eventually dying of exhaustion or suffocation.

Sundews can move!

Though not as quickly as the snap-trap Venus' Flytrap, the leaves and tentacles of most sundews can move. In some species, a leaf will fold over the struggling prey in a matter of minutes.

Their natural home

In Europe and North America, sundews are mainly found in peat bogs, which are ancient, acidic wetlands formed from rotting bog moss (called *Sphagnum*) that accumulates in deep layers. In places like Australia, parts of Africa and South America, they are usually found in sandy or rocky soils that get plenty of rain for at least part of the year. What they have in common is that the soil they grow in is very poor – most other plants wouldn't survive such habitats!

How these plants feed

Sundews don't hide a thing – the insects they catch are digested right on the surface of the leaves by digestive juices produced by special cells. The released nutrients are absorbed by the plant.

The tentacles of sundews are very specialised. In addition to producing the glue that they use to snare insects, some species are able to reposition prey for more efficient digestion. In pygmy sundews, some tentacles are able to flick prey right into the middle of the leaf – a really deadly smackdown!

ATTRACTING PREY

Sundews are experts at catching small prey. It is believed that insects are attracted to the deadly leaves of the plants by the sparkling drops of glue and bright coloration. However, some species also smell sweet, and may lure in prey with the promise of nectar.

Flypaper traps 25

BUTTERWORTS
(Pinguicula)

Like sundews, butterworts have leaves covered in tentacles, but the tentacles of butterworts are much smaller and more numerous. They usually catch slightly smaller prey, though larger animals like crane flies are sometimes overwhelmed by the sticky glue, quickly drowning on the surface of the leaves.

Their natural home

Butterworts are unusual among carnivorous plants because many species — especially those from Central America — occur in habitats that seem relatively dry. These species are actually adapted to survive distinct wet and dry seasons, while their cousins from more northern areas like the US, Canada and Europe are a little more typical: like most carnivorous plants, they prefer wet conditions and frequently occur in bogs or alongside streams and lakes.

Attracting prey

Butterworts rely on a similar mechanism to sundews when attracting prey. Their leaves glisten brightly in sunlight and even sparkle on overcast days, which may attract insects. Their leaves also appear smooth and flat, and probably look like great places to rest!

How these plants feed

Like sundews, butterworts digest insects in the open air. While their leaves don't move dramatically, they can curl to form a pool of digestive acid when the prey are trapped.

BUTTERWORTS HAVE BEAUTIFUL FLOWERS

Many people grow carnivorous plants because they are interesting to look at, but butterworts are also grown for their flowers, especially by orchid lovers who use them to trap insect pests.

Butterworts are some of the easiest carnivorous plants to grow on a windowsill, so they are a good choice for the first-time grower of carnivorous plants. With their fleshy leaves, they can even tolerate the occasional missed watering, though of course they won't be happy left unwatered for long.

Flypaper traps 27

BLADDERWORTS
(Utricularia)

Many people don't realise that harmless-looking bladderworts are carnivorous. Most species have tiny, grass-like leaves that can almost disappear from view, even amongst small mosses, with the plants only becoming obvious when they flower. Their carnivorous traps are mostly underground or aquatic, but can easily be uncovered for a look.

Their natural home

Bladderworts occur in a range of wet, or seasonally wet, habitats. Many species float free in water, sometimes amongst reeds. These can be found from areas with cold winters all the way to the equator. Other species are terrestrial, growing in wet soil, amongst moss or even over rocks. Most species are found in tropical and subtropical regions in savannah and swamps, but many can survive colder habitats by going dormant in winter, rather like many deciduous trees do by dropping their leaves.

How these plants feed

The bladder traps of bladderworts actively suck in prey that swim past when they strike tiny hairs that surround the closed door of the trap. Once the hairs are touched, the door springs open and the bladder inflates, pulling in water and anything swimming in it. The door then closes and animals caught inside are flooded with digestive juices. It's rather similar to the stomachs of animals.

ORCHIDS OF THE CARNIVOROUS PLANT WORLD

Like butterworts, the bladderworts have beautiful flowers. However, the flowers are so stunning – and can be so large – that they are often referred to as the orchids of the carnivorous plant world. Most bladderworts actually produce rather small flowers, but these can be as exquisite as tiny jewels.

Attracting prey

Prey attraction in bladderworts is not perfectly understood. It is assumed that animals simply blunder into the traps, rather than being lured there. This might explain why the plants produce hundreds of traps, making an encounter with prey much more likely!

TROPICAL PITCHER PLANTS
(Nepenthes)

Tropical pitcher plants produce the largest traps of all carnivorous plants, and you just can't miss them. The traps form from the elongated tips of the leaves, and the vines they grow on may climb metres into the canopy. Each pitcher has a lid and, usually, a mouth surrounded by a ridged structure bearing teeth of variable sizes.

Their natural home

Over 130 tropical pitcher plant species have been named from Southeast Asia, with just a handful of other species occurring from Madagascar to India. All grow in humid and more or less permanently damp habitats, though some are only suited to the hot lowlands, while others flourish in cold, mossy cloud forests at the tops of mountains.

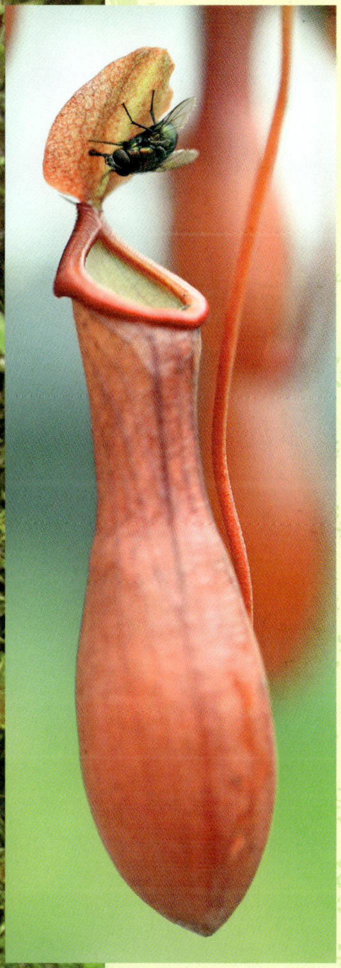

Attracting prey

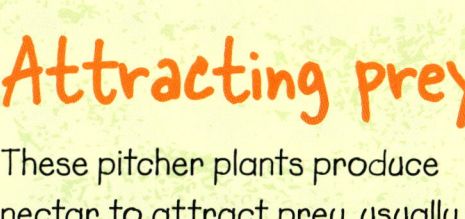

These pitcher plants produce nectar to attract prey, usually under their pitcher lids or on the margins of the ridged mouth. Insects hanging around on either surface are in a dangerous position. One slip, and they're done for! The surface of the mouth is ultra-slippery, so slippery, in fact, that materials scientists are copying it to create surfaces that dust and dirt won't stick to! The inside of the pitchers may also have a waxy layer that peels off, coating the feet of prey and stopping them from climbing out.

PITCHER PERFECT!

Tropical pitcher plant traps come in all shapes and sizes. Some species aren't carnivorous at all – instead, they eat animal poop!

How these plants feed

Tropical pitcher plants contain a watery liquid rich in digestive acids and enzymes (proteins that speed digestion). Any prey falling in is simply digested in a matter of weeks, sometimes in days!

The giant *Nepenthes rajah* (page 23) and toilet-shaped *N. lowii* (left) both have upright lids that allow small mammals like tree shrews to feed from them. These animals rarely end up as food, but regularly poop while drinking from the pitchers. Anything they produce falls straight into the pitcher below, providing the plants with nutrients!

Pitfall traps 31

NORTH AMERICAN PITCHER PLANTS
(Sarracenia)

These pitcher plants are found only in North America. Unlike the tropical pitcher plants, the entire leaf forms the pitcher trap. Each leaf develops from a short, horizontal stem that grows along the ground. The pitchers emerge directly from this stem and grow upwards or outwards, depending on the species.

THEIR NATURAL HOME

The North American pitcher plants are all bog species. Almost all of them are found in the south-eastern United States, where they occur in an arc from eastern Texas through southern Mississippi to Florida, and north through Georgia to Virginia. One species also occurs further inland and further north than all others, reaching the Great Lakes in southern Canada.

Attracting prey

These pitcher plants produce great quantities of sweet nectar around the lid and mouth. Their bright colours are also thought to attract visitors of all kinds.

DRUGS FOR INSECTS

The nectar produced by these pitcher plants contains a narcotic drug. This substance effectively makes insects drunk, a little bit clumsy and much more likely to fall in to their death!

How these plants feed

Like the tropical pitcher plants, these species produce a fluid containing digestive acids and enzymes. The pitcher walls are also variably covered with rows of downward-pointing hairs. Along with the waxy, smooth walls, these hairs make climbing out very difficult, especially for winged insects.

The North American pitcher plants are some of the most effective of all carnivorous plants. It is not unusual for an entire pitcher to fill up with insects over the course of one growing season. They are so successful that many types of animal, including spiders and tree frogs, may live on or inside pitchers so that they can grab a free snack from within whenever they become hungry.

Pitfall traps 33

MARSH PITCHER PLANTS (Heliamphora)

Marsh pitcher plants are found only in South America and are very closely related to the North American pitcher plants. These pitcher plants look simpler than their northern cousins, with their pitchers more obviously formed from rolled leaves, and their small lids leaving them open to the rain.

That's hairy effective!

Like the northern pitcher plants, marsh pitcher plants produce rows of downward-pointing hairs on their inner walls. This is very effective at stopping trapped prey from escaping.

Carnivorous plants

Attracting prey

The marsh pitcher plants produce sweet nectar beneath their small lid. Insects can only feed from the lid by positioning themselves under it, right on the slippery, vertical wall of the pitcher!

The marsh pitcher plants include some of the most beautiful traps of all, being elegantly waisted in the middle. They also produce very pretty flowers on tall, red flower stems that tower above the traps. In this way, the plants reduce the chances of trapping insects that come to pollinate their flowers, as they depend on these insects to help them produce seed. So eating them would be no good at all!

Their natural home

The marsh pitcher plants are some of the most difficult carnivorous plants to visit. Most species occur on table mountains in the far north of South America, particularly Venezuela and Brazil. These mountains have vertical walls 1 kilometre high and their cold, flat tops are called 'rain deserts' — this is because there is so much rain at the tops of these mountains that most of the soil and almost all of the nutrients are washed away! The plants that survive in this habitat are usually found nowhere else on Earth.

How these plants feed

They really are primitive: some species don't even produce digestive juices — instead they rely on bacteria to break down their prey and absorb whatever is released into the pitcher fluid.

ALBANY PITCHER PLANT
(Cephalotus follicularis)

Australia's Albany Pitcher Plant is one of the cutest of all pitcher plant species. It produces two types of leaves: the first are small, flat and oval like those of many other plants, while the second type are the carnivorous pitcher leaves. Both types of leaf are produced in a compact rosette from a short, ground-hugging stem.

Their natural home

The Albany Pitcher Plant is one of the most endangered pitcher plants in the world. It occurs in a very small range centred more or less on the town of Albany in the south-west of Western Australia. It grows in permanently damp beds of acidic peat soil mixed with variable amounts of sand. The plants are often found growing beneath larger shrubs or marsh grasses, often in deep shade that few other plants would survive.

Attracting prey

The Albany Pitcher Plant produces nectar from small nectaries around the toothed pitcher rim. Coupled with the hair-lined ridges that guide insects up towards the pitcher mouth, this strategy can be quite effective at trapping crawling insects.

How these plants feed

This little pitcher plant produces a number of acids and enzymes that are capable of rapidly breaking down prey. This fate awaits any insect that falls into the fluid bath within the pitcher.

The lid of the Albany Pitcher Plant has white patches on it that allow light to pass through. It is believed that insects crawling up the pitcher are attracted towards the bright patches beneath the lid, slightly increasing the chances of being caught. Once there, escape is prevented by the rim of teeth around the pitcher mouth, as well as by microscopic downward-pointing hairs within.

THAT LID DOESN'T MOVE!

Many people believe that the lids of pitcher plants close. Actually, no pitcher plants anywhere produce a moving lid. They usually serve to keep out rain and to attract prey.

Pitfall traps

VENUS' FLYTRAP
(Dionaea muscipula)

Arguably the world's most famous carnivorous plant, the Venus' Flytrap, is unmistakable. With its dramatic-looking toothed leaves and high-speed snap-trap action, it is easy to understand why this is one of the most popular plants amongst young plant lovers. Sadly, many end up dead, but they're easy to grow once you know how!

Their natural home

The Venus' Flytrap occurs naturally only on the coastal plains of North and South Carolina, in the United States, where it grows in wet pine savannahs. Populations today are far lower than they used to be as a result of habitat loss. Sadly, many plants are also illegally removed from the wild to sell for just a few dollars each, threatening their survival. Fortunately, this species is produced in great numbers commercially, helping to take some of the pressure off wild-collected plants.

38 Carnivorous plants

Attracting prey

The *Venus' Flytrap* evolved to capture mainly crawling prey such as beetles and ants. These are attracted to the trapping leaves by the presence of small nectar-producing glands along their edges. So it possibly should have been called the Venus' Beetletrap!

How these plants feed

Once the trap closes on its prey, the toothed edges of the leaf are shut together hard, forming a seal. The space inside then fills with digestive juices that rapidly break down prey.

Venus' Flytraps can count!

In order for a Venus' Flytrap to close, any one of the six trigger hairs present in the trap (three on each half) must be touched twice within about 10–20 seconds. If touched once, the trap won't close! It is believed that the traps require two trigger events to close to save energy: false-alarms like falling leaves are not as likely to trigger the hairs twice as animals are. Once closed, the trap won't start digesting unless the hairs are triggered about five more times by trapped insects. They really can count!

Snap traps 39

How to Grow

Many species of carnivorous plant are easy to grow. The key is to choose species that will grow well in the conditions that you can offer them. In the wild, carnivorous plants grow in acidic peat and other nutrient-poor soils. In cultivation, the use of horticultural peat is often recommended, however this contributes to the destruction of rare peat bogs and should be avoided. Environmentally friendly peat products, such as Moorland Gold (which is produced as a by-product of the water industry and doesn't harm peat bogs) works really well as a substitute for horticultural peat and is recommended for many carnivorous plants.

You generally need:

1. Soil – the best general soil is an equal mix of peat, perlite and sand containing no fertiliser at all. A good nursery will be able to recommend some products for you.
2. Pots 8–10cm in diameter and 10cm high for small to medium sized plants.
3. A plastic tray to stand the pots in. This should have no holes so that your pots can stand in water if necessary.
4. Plants that will grow well in your conditions.

Soil

One reason many people lose their first Venus' Flytrap is because the plants are often sold in poor soil. Carnivorous plants like damp to wet soil, which can lead to rapid rotting and death if the soil is not of good quality. If you buy your first carnivorous plants from a specialist nursery, you should be fine, but hardware store carnivorous plants often need to be repotted immediately. The peat-perlite-sand mix recommended above works for many species!

Water

Carnivorous plants require extremely clean water. For many people, tap water contains too many harmful chemicals, and is often not acidic enough. Rainwater is the best source of suitable water and can easily be collected. Failing that, look for a source of distilled or 'reverse osmosis' water – filtered water is not suitable. In warm weather (such as in spring and summer), many of the most popular carnivorous plant species should be stood in 2–3cm of water all the time. This makes watering easy! In winter, wet conditions can lead to rot: reduce water levels so that the soil stays just damp, and provide as much ventilation as you can.

Temperatures

Most carnivorous plants will grow well in the 22–28°C temperature range in summer. Tropical species (like tropical pitcher plants) will require similar temperatures throughout the winter, whereas species from regions with cold winters may go dormant or at least slow their growth in winter. For those species, temperatures around 4–8°C in winter are beneficial. This is true of the North American pitcher plants and the Venus' Flytrap. Many sundews and butterworts benefit from a cool winter (about 15–18°C), which can often be achieved on a windowsill. Always check with your supplier or online for your particular species.

BEST CARNIVOROUS PLANTS FOR THE BEGINNER

A few different species are recommended for those new to growing carnivorous plants. Each species is described using its scientific name – you'll get to learn these quickly if you get the 'carnivorous plant bug', so don't worry too much if they seem confusing! Most of those recommended require a cool or cold winter, but those tolerating a warm winter are indicated.

Sundews

These species grow well in equal parts of peat/perlite/sand.

Drosera capensis: a vigorous and easy to grow upright species with long, arching leaves. This species is easy to propagate from seed and root cuttings. Cape region, South Africa. Cool to warm winter.

Drosera aliciae: a vigorous and easy to grow rosetted species forming attractive cushions of leaves. This species is also easily propagated by seed, as well as leaf and root cuttings. Cape region, South Africa. Cool to warm winter.

Drosera spatulata: an easy to grow rosetted species with spoon-like leaves. This species ranges from eastern Asia through to Australia and New Zealand. Cool to warm winter.

Drosera regia: a large and moderately easy to grow species, so long as you don't let it overheat in summer. It has large, arching leaves and may form clumps over the years. Cape region, South Africa. Cool winter.

Drosera roraimae: this species produces semi-erect rosettes of leaves, and forms upright stems after a few years of continued growth. This moderately easy species is native to South America. Cool to warm winter.

Drosera slackii: a moderately easy rosetted species with robust, handsome leaves forming large rosettes. This species is easily propagated by leaf and root cuttings. Cape region, South Africa. Cool to warm winter.

HOW TO GROW

Sundews 41

Butterworts

Pinguicula primuliflora: a prolific and rapidly dividing species with lovely pinkish flowers. This North American plant is easily propagated by leaf and root cuttings. Wet throughout the year. South-eastern United States. Cool to warm winter.

Pinguicula moranensis: a beautiful plant with large, fleshy summer leaves and orchid-like flowers. Must be kept slightly drier in winter. Grow in equal parts perlite and vermiculite. Mexico and Guatemala. Cool winter.

Pinguicula esseriana: a diminutive but tough species with jewel-like leaves and frequent flowers. Must be kept slightly drier in winter. Grow in equal parts perlite and vermiculite. Mexico. Cool winter.

Pinguicula gigantea: a large species with succulent looking leaves and large flowers. Must be kept dry in winter. Grow in equal parts perlite and vermiculite. Oaxaca, Mexico. Cool winter.

Pinguicula* x *kewensis: a vigorous hybrid plant with multiple beautiful flowers. Must be kept slightly drier in winter. Grow in equal parts perlite and vermiculite. This hybrid was bred at the Royal Botanic Gardens Kew. Cool winter.

***Pinguicula* cv 'Weser'**: is a German cultivar of a cross between *P. moranensis* and *P. ehlersiae*. Must be kept slightly drier in winter. Grow in equal parts perlite and vermiculite. This hybrid was named after the River Weser, Germany. Cool winter.

Bladderworts

Grow all in equal parts peat/sand.

Utricularia gibba: this aquatic species should be grown in shallow water overlying peat all year. The traps are easy to observe since they are not hidden in soil. It produces yellow flowers. It occurs worldwide in the tropics, but prefers cool winter conditions.

Utricularia livida: a free flowering and easy to grow species. It produces elegant, light purple flowers and blooms en masse. It originates from tropical and sub-tropical regions of Africa, and grows well as a windowsill plant or in a terrarium.

Utricularia sandersonii: this tiny species produces surprisingly large stems bearing masses of pretty flowers. It is easy to grow and will quickly colonise a pot. It can be kept wet all year round. It originates from South Africa and grows very well on a windowsill.

Venus' Flytrap

An equal mix of peat/perlite/sand is ideal.

Dionaea muscipula: there is only one species of Venus' Flytrap. This plant is relatively easy to provided with the right conditions.

Ensure that it is planted in an acidic, nutrient-free soil like moss peat, with added perlite and sand for improved drainage. During the spring and summer, stand the pot in a few centimetres of water to keep the soil wet. In winter, the soil should not be allowed to dry out, but watering can be reduced to keep the dormant plant just damp. Water must be very pure, as for most other carnivorous plants, rainwater being the most easily accessible water of suitable quality. The Venus' Flytrap benefits from annual repotting while it is dormant. The best time to do this is before growth resumes in the spring.

It comes from North and South Carolina, USA.
Cool to cold winter.

HOW TO GROW

Butterworts, bladderworts and Venus' Flytrap 43

Tropical Pitcher Plants

Some species require warm winters, others cool winters, but always above 15°C. A more open soil of equal parts peat/perlite/medium orchid bark is ideal. The plants will only produce pitchers if the air is humid (70+%), which may require a tank or greenhouse.

Nepenthes ventricosa: an unusual species with waxy-looking, elegant pitchers. It is one of the most forgiving of all *Nepenthes* species, its hybrids even more so. Keep damp, not wet, throughout the year. Philippines. Cool winter.

Nepenthes maxima: a large and beautiful species with strikingly patterned pitchers. A vigorous grower as long as conditions are not too warm. Keep damp throughout the year. Indonesia. Cool winter.

Nepenthes rafflesiana: a fast growing and very handsome species with incredible looking pitchers. It is one of the easiest lowland *Nepenthes* species to grow and can tolerate wet conditions. Malaysia, Singapore and Indonesia. Warm winter.

North American Pitcher Plants

The plants all do well in an equal mix of peat/perlite/sand.

Sarracenia flava: an upright species with large, trumpet-like, yellowish-green pitchers marked with red. Pitchers may reach almost 1 metre in height. Wet during the spring and summer, damp when dormant. Cool winter.

Sarracenia leucophylla: a beautiful species with elegant pitchers topped with white and variable amounts of red. This species produces a flush of pitchers in the spring, and again in Autumn. Cool winter.

Sarracenia purpurea subspecies **venosa**: a squat species with broad, belly-like pitchers that form a rosette close to the ground. Generally very forgiving, tolerating wet conditions throughout the year. Cool to cold winter.

Marsh Pitcher Plants

Heliamphora are not generally recommended for the beginner. Try growing only if you are successful with other carnivorous plants.

Heliamphora nutans and **H. heterodoxa** are the most forgiving. These species both produce beautiful pitchers and are will tolerate higher temperatures than other species. The secret, if you hadn't guessed, is to keep them cool, a daytime maximum temperature of 23°C year-round should be your goal. Venezuela. Cool winter, do not allow temperatures to fall below 8°C.

Albany Pitcher Plant

Cephalotus follicularis is the only species in this genus. It is generally easy to grow, requiring damp conditions year round, though not happy for long in stagnant standing water. Some growers water from above, others by tray, but if using tray, open up the soil by adding perlite. Otherwise, equal parts peat/perlite are suitable. Albany, Australia. It produces pitcher leaves mainly in winter (cool winter) when it should be kept damp as it will still be in growth.

How to grow

Tropical, North American, marsh and Albany pitcher plants 45

Unbelievable Flowers

The first recognisable land plants evolved at least 390 million years ago, but the first true flowers did not appear until around 200 million years ago. At around 50 million years ago, many flowering plants evolved that had blooms which actively attracted pollinators, which enabled pollen to be carried from one plant to another. This may not seem very significant, but it was one of the most important milestones in the evolution of life on Earth.

Suddenly, individual plants could exchange genetic information very efficiently, this led to an explosion of plant types, with millions of new flowering plant species evolving.

Today, our world is home to at least 500,000 species of flowering plants that occur in an amazing range of shapes, colours and sizes. Flowers can be found on all continents and almost all islands scattered across the planet.

BIGGEST FLOWER IN THE WORLD?

To discover the world's largest bloom, we first have to define how we classify a flower. The flowers of some plants fit the stereotype of a round circle surrounded by colourful semi-circular petals. But in other species, the 'flower' can consist of a flower scape made up of lots of little flowers (sometimes called florets) positioned together. Flower scapes can be branched or unbranched.

single flower

branched flower scape

unbranched flower scape

LARGEST SINGLE FLOWER

The plant with the largest single bloom is a corpse flower (see also *Rafflesia* in the World's Smelliest Flowers chapter, page 73). There are many species of corpse flower, but one called *Rafflesia arnoldii*, that grows in the steamy jungles of *Sumatra* (an island off Indonesia), produces flowers that are over one metre wide and can weigh over 10kg! Like all corpse flowers, the gigantic bloom lasts for only a few days before it dies and rots.

The corpse flower is a really bizarre plant. It doesn't have any leaves or roots, but grows as a parasite inside a tropical vine called *Tetrastigma*. The corpse flower steals all of the energy it needs to produce its gigantic flower.

Unfortunately, this specialised life cycle makes the corpse flower almost impossible to grow, because to grow the corpse flower, you first have to grow a tropical vine. But no one has really worked out how to infect the vine with corpse flower seeds!

one metre across

10kg = 10 bags of flour!

48 Unbelievable flowers

LARGEST BRANCHED FLOWER SCAPE

While the corpse flower may produce the largest single bloom in the plant kingdom, many other plant species produce flower scapes that are much larger, carrying many smaller individual flowers.

The record for the largest flower scape of all belongs to the Talipot Palm (*Corypha umbraculifera*) from southern Indian and Sri Lanka. This huge palm grows to over 25m tall, with a stem over 1m wide. It grows for up to 60 years, then produces a gigantic flower scape up to 8m long, which can have up to several million tiny flowers.

Amazingly, each Talipot Palm produces just one flower scape in its lifetime; as once the fruit are ripened, carrying the seeds of the next generation, the plant dies.

Like many palm species, the Talipot Palm is easy to grow, but due to its massive size, it is almost impossible to grow outside of gardens in the tropics!

each one up to eight metres long

Largest flowers 49

LARGEST UNBRANCHED FLOWER SCAPE

Two groups of plants rival each other for the title of the world's largest unbranched flower scape. The Titan Arum (*Amorphophallus titanum*) produces a monster bloom that can tower over 3m in height and over 1.5m in width. In this species, two rings of hundreds of small flowers are positioned (a ring of male flowers above a ring of female ones). The hundreds of little flowers are grouped together inside a gigantic bell-shaped, dark red petal (called the spathe), out of which towers a huge chimney-like structure called the spadix.

This enormous flower stinks like rotting meat to attract pollinators that feed on dead animals and, during flowering, the tip of the spadix actually warms up to about human body temperature to help the stench spread into the air!

The Titan Arum produces just one leaf a year, but each leaf can be the size of a small tree! Despite the enormous size, the Titan Arum can be grown in cultivation in a similar way to the Devil's Tongue Plant (the World's Smelliest Flowers chapter, page 91). But most Titan Arums take at least seven years to grow before they are large enough to flower.

Unbelievable flowers

over three metres high

one and a half metres wide

In 2011, Roseville High School in California became the first school in the world to successfully bloom a Titan Arum. No school in the UK has yet flowered one. So ask your teachers if your school can make plant history by flowering this gigantic arum!

The Titan Arum has a far less well-known cousin called *Amorphophallus gigas*. In this species, the flower is smaller (generally 1.5m or less), but it grows on an enormous stem that can be up to 5m tall, so that the resulting structure can be taller than a lamp post! This great height allows the flower's smell to spread further in the rainforest.

THAT'S ONE BIG POT PLANT!

The Titan Arum is so huge that it has to be grown in a pot that is at least 1.5 metres wide! It also has a giant underground tuber, called a corm, that stores energy like a potato. Gardeners at the Royal Botanic Garden Edinburgh hold the world record for the biggest ever corm. They planted a Titan Arum that had a corm the size of an orange, and seven years later, with the help of scales borrowed from Edinburgh Zoo, the corm weighed in at a massive 153.9kg!

Largest flowers

QUEEN OF THE ANDES

Bromeliads are usually small, colourful plants that often grow on the branches of trees (see World's Most Spectacular Plants chapter, page 138). But on rocky slopes above 3,000m high in the Andes Mountains of South America, there grows the world's largest species of bromeliad. This monster plant is known locally as the Queen of the Andes, and to scientists as *Puya raimondii*. It produces giant balls of spiky leaves up to 3m across on a trunk up to 5m tall. When it flowers the unbranched flower scape can be 8m tall, so the plant may tower 16m or more above the ground. Each flower scape can produce up to 20,000 flowers!

Unbelievable flowers

up to eight metres high

SHEEP-EATING PLANT

The Queen of the Andes has a close relative called *Puya chilensis*. This species produces leaves that are smaller, but covered with ferocious spines. Birds and even sheep become entangled in the spines of the leaves, and many cases have been reported of the animals dying amongst the leaves. Local sheep farmers have given it the nickname 'sheep-eating plant', and some farmers hate the plant so much that they burn it whenever they can, to protect their sheep. Sadly, this makes the 'sheep-eating plant' ever rarer in its natural habitat!

spiky!

Queen of the Andes 53

FACES IN THE FLOWERS

The majority of flowers have both male parts (usually stamens which carry pollen-bearing anthers), and female parts (sticky stigmas which receive the pollen in order for the flower to be fertilised). In some species, individual plants may be male or female, and produce only one type of flower.

As a means of reproducing, flowers have evolved into a myriad of amazing shapes, sizes and colours. Out of the hundreds of thousands of different flowers, some just happen to resemble other things. These lookalike flowers did not evolve to please us humans. Rather, they are the result of flowers evolving to attract different pollinators (usually insects such as bees or birds like hummingbirds) by offering them drinks of tasty nectar in the most persuasive way they can.

Of the amazing diversity of plants on our planet, orchids are one of the most varied groups of all, and the flowers of several orchid species take amusing forms.

54 Unbelievable flowers

Oncidium orchids from the Americas often resemble dancing ladies with petticoats, whereas the many *Orchis* species from Europe and Asia produce flowers that look just like dancing, naked men!

Perhaps most incredible of all is a plant called *Impatiens bequaertii* (right). This miniature species of balsam hails from the rainforests of the Congo, Burundi and Rwanda in central to east Africa. The plants creep across the ground, putting roots down wherever their stems touch the soil, but they only grow to about 20cm in each direction. What makes them special is their amazing little flowers. Just 1.5cm long, the white to pale pink blooms resemble little girls – wearing ballet dresses and hats – with their arms outstretched. It is no surprise that they have earned the common name 'dancing girls'!

Faces in the flowers 55

The White Egret Orchid (*Habenaria radiata*) produces blooms that look a lot like flying egrets.

In Australia, the Flying Duck Orchid (*Caleana major*) has complex little duck-shaped blooms that evolved to attract wasps, whereas South America's Monkey Face Orchid (*Dracula simia*) (photo page 54) and several other related species have flowers which look as though they have a monkey face staring out of them!

In the Falkland Islands, Lady's Slipper Flowers (*Calceolaria fothergillii*) grow on rocky slopes. The blooms of this species do look like slippers, but also resemble a bizarre, gaping face with googly eyes!

Unbelievable flowers

HOW TO GROW

It is true that many of the most unusual looking flowers with faces are rare or difficult to grow, but not all of them. One of the easiest flowers with face-like markings is the pansy, which most flower seed sellers stock a range of varieties. They grow easily outdoors in your garden, or in a pot or window box – all they need is good quality potting soil, a light sprinkling of water every few days, and plenty of sun.

If you want to try other human-mimicking plants, you might consider the following:

Monkey Face Orchid

Dracula simia has strange, three-pointed flowers that resemble the face of a monkey (see photo page 54). This species hails from the rainforests of the Andes mountains in South America. The secret to growing it successfully is to remember where it came from: keep it COOL! This makes it perfect for the UK, where our occasionally rubbish summers are actually really good for plants! Monkey Face Orchids actually grow quite easily just so long as you give them days of 18–20°C, with a nice drop to about 8–15°C at night, with high humidity and bright shade. This makes them a great plant for the cool conservatory or humid bathroom. For soil, they do best in a freely draining pot or mesh basket filled with fine orchid bark that should be kept damp.

Impatiens bequaertii

Although this species was first described in 1922, people have only recently started growing it, which means that it is still tricky to find. The good news is that 'dancing girls' plants are easy to grow indoors on ordinary, well-drained potting soil, provided you can offer them warmth (20–28°C), with a humid atmosphere (50–80%) and bright, filtered light. They come from the damp understorey of the rainforest, after all! While most other *Impatiens* species don't have flowers that look like dancing girls (elephant's trunks and birds are more common), many are easy growing and very beautiful.

Skull pod snapdragon

Antirrhinum majus is a popular garden flower, coming in many beautiful varieties (left). But its seed pods couldn't be more different – they look like moaning skulls with large foreheads! (see page 59) The good news is that they're easy to grow, and will please those who love beautiful things just as much as those who love gruesome-looking things. Like pansies, these tough plants do best outside in a flower bed, pot or window box. They prefer a sunny spot with damp, freely draining potting mix and temperatures of 10–30°C in summer.

The Devil's Hand

Chiranthodendron pentadactylon is a tropical mountain species from Guatemala with some seriously weird flowers. These don't have a face, this time, but a rather creepy, thin-fingered hand, which emerges from a blood-red cup of nectar, each finger ending in a lethal looking claw! These plants can actually be grown outdoors in warmer areas, but since they don't like temperatures below 5°C, they are best kept in a cool conservatory in bright light, with good quality potting mix and damp soil. Established plants can tolerate brief spells below freezing, but only if their soil is relatively dry.

Faces in the flowers 57

SCARY FLOWERS

Some plants have flowers that look scary. The Darth Vader Flower (*Aristolochia salvadorensis*) (right) is a tropical vine that produces flowers that hang in mid-air and resemble the helmets of the evil cyborg ruler from Star Wars. The little helmet flowers even have two pale eye-sockets! Whereas the seed pods of several *Antirrhinum* species resemble skulls!

In South America, there is a group of orchids called *Dracula*, an allusion to the mythical Count Dracula of vampire novels and films. The orchids were given this name because several produce flowers that are blood-red in colour and have long, fang-like spurs on their sepals. There is one species with black striped flowers called *Dracula vampira* (below), as it looks particularly scary and vampire-like!

58 Unbelievable flowers

HOW TO GROW

Aristolochia

Aristolochia salvadorensis plants are occasionally sold online, especially via eBay, but because they're so unusual, they sell out quickly. The good news is that they are relatively easy to grow in a large pot provided you can keep them warm. They are native to Guatemala and Honduras, and do best in warm temperatures of 18–28°C with a minimum of about 12°C. For this reason, they are best in a warm conservatory or very bright room with reasonably high humidity. For equally weird-looking flowers, take a look at *Aristolochia fimbriata*, *A. cymbifera* (below) and *A. tiracambu*, which look like carnivorous pitcher plants and will grow easily, as long as you keep them above 12°C and give them plenty of sunshine.

Dracula

Dracula are actually some of the most popular South American orchids grown in north-western Europe, since they like cool temperatures. As a result, it's possible to find many different species, including *D. vampira*, but also a huge number of easy to grow, funereal-looking hybrids. Like the Monkey Face Orchid *Dracula simia* (see page 57), many species of *Dracula* are easy to grow just so long as you keep them cool and moist. That is, 18–20°C in the day, with a night-time drop to about 8–15°C, with high humidity and bright shade. Most tropical orchids grow happily in good quality orchid bark.

Antirrhinum majus seed pods

scary flowers

HOT LIPS FLOWER

Other plants have blooms which take on funny shapes. The Hot Lips Flower (*Psychotria elata*) produces bright red, puckered lips that look as if they are about to give a smooch! The lips are the plant's flower, or more accurately, they consist of a pair of red bracts (modified leaves), out of which tiny, star-shaped flowers emerge which attract butterflies and hummingbirds.

HOW TO GROW

Psychotria elata occurs in Central America, ranging from southern Mexico to northern Colombia. As a tropical species, it fares best in warm conditions of 20–28°C, though it can tolerate temperatures below 12°C for short periods. Plants should be kept damp in a rich, good quality potting compost, and be situated in a spot that is humid (50–80%). The plants should get plenty of bright light, though for young plants, direct sun for more than a couple of hours per day should be avoided to prevent leaf burn.

After becoming 'internet famous' for its lip-like flower bracts, this species has become hard to find and many online sellers sell fake seeds for a quick buck. It is best to look for this plant from reputable sellers only.

60 Unbelievable flowers

4 O'CLOCK FLOWER

Some plants have evolved flowers that have specialised not just their shapes and colours, but also what time their blooms open in order to attract pollinators. The Four O'Clock Flower (*Mirabilis jalapa*) produces blooms that open from late afternoon (around 4pm) onwards, and then produce a strong, sweet-smelling fragrance throughout the night to attract nocturnal pollinators (particularly moths), before closing the next morning.

Interestingly, the Four O'Clock Flower produces trumpet-shaped blooms with different colours growing simultaneously on the same plant, and each individual flower can be splashed with different combinations of red, yellow, pink, or white.

HOW TO GROW

It is a very easy plant to grow, and is available to buy as seeds from most garden centres. Sow the seeds in a light but rich, well composted, soil, and keep moist, in a warm, sunny location. The seeds will germinate quickly (usually within two weeks), and the young plants will grow quickly. You can plant your Four O'Clock Flower plants straight into flower beds in your garden (for summer growth), or in pots if you wish to grow them for more than one year.

Choose a site for your young plants in full sunlight (as this species becomes lanky and doesn't flower as readily in shaded conditions), ensure that the soil doesn't ever dry out or become waterlogged, apply slow-release fertiliser and give liquid fertiliser once a month to encourage vigorous flowering.

Once your Four O'Clock Flower starts to bloom, you can time it and see if your flowers are on time, opening at exactly 4pm. On cloudy days, sometimes the flowers open a little later.

Hot Lips & Four O'Clock flowers

BAT FLOWERS

Lurking in the shadows of the tropical rainforest, the Black Bat Flower (*Tacca chantrieri*) has one of the most bizarre flowers of all plants. It originates from Southeast Asia and China along with several other closely related species.

The flower scape is dark purple, maroon or black, and consists of two pairs of bat wing-like bracts with thread-like whiskers growing beneath them, known as bracteoles. Up to 25 small, round flowers emerge on stalks, and point upwards when they are open, then droop downwards when they have finished flowering. The whole structure may be up to 50cm tall and 30cm wide.

No one is really sure why the flowers are shaped in the bizarre bat-like way that they are. Some botanists believe that the colour and shape of the flowers resemble rotting organic material to attract flies. Others have suggested that the strange shape of the flower evolved to enable self pollination. A last theory is that the whiskers allow ants to climb up to the flowers and cross-pollinate them.

Whatever the reason for its unusual flowers, the bat flower plant is easy to grow at home. While you can grow bat flowers from seeds, for the best results, buy a large, healthy, established plant which is likely to flower quickly for you.

In the wild, bat flowers are understorey plants, growing in dank and shady conditions in the rainforest, so in captivity, they prefer shade (at least 40% shaded conditions), and grow best when protected from direct sunlight.

Unbelievable flowers

HOW TO GROW

This need for low light levels makes bat flowers very suitable for cultivation indoors, for example, on a kitchen windowsill. Make sure conditions stay above 5°C, and plant the bat flower in light, loam-rich, nutritious soil with excellent drainage, which is critical for *Tacca*. Orchid potting mixes work well for the bat plant, often with added perlite to ensure that the soil drains very effectively. Keep the soil moist, but not wet (which can cause rotting). Water twice a week or so during the growing season, and make sure humidity levels remain high (and spray with a mister, if needed). To encourage flowering, use slow-release fertiliser pellets, and apply a liquid fertiliser every two weeks during the growing season.

If you follow all of these requirements, this remarkable plant should grow rapidly and flower many times each year over many years to come!

BIRD OF PARADISE FLOWER

The Bird of Paradise Flower (*Strelizia reginae*) from South Africa has an even more flamboyant flower than the bat flower plants. It is so called because of a resemblance of its flowers to the birds of paradise of New Guinea, however it is pollinated by sunbirds.

Bat flowers

LOBSTER CLAW FLOWERS

The Bird of Paradise Flower is not the only plant species that evolved to use birds as pollinators. Hummingbirds often migrate vast distances across the Americas, and need to drink nectar regularly to refuel with energy. One group of plants called *Heliconia*, from the Americas, have evolved to be hummingbird fueling stations, and have flowers that are adapted perfectly to suit their curved beaks. In many *Heliconia*, the hummingbird is able to perch on a flower, and as it reaches into the nectaries to drink the honey-sweet nectar, the plant deposits a dab of pollen on the top of its head, so that the next time it visits a flower, it delivers the pollen and fertilises the bloom.

Some *Heliconia* flowers produce blooms reminiscent of an upright Bird of Paradise Flower, while others arrange their flowers in spectacular groups that can hang together in rows and measure 1 metre or more! The flowers of one species look just like red lobster claws!

Sunbirds visit the Bird of Paradise Flower, sometimes using the blue stamen as a perch to stand on while licking nectar from its base. The weight of the bird standing on the stamen causes it to split open and release pollen onto the bird's feet. When the bird flies to the next flower, it deposits pollen on the white, sticky stigma located at the tip of the stamen.

Unbelievable flowers

HOW TO GROW

Bird of Paradise (*Strelizia reginae*) and lobster claw (*Heliconia*) flowers can be grown under the same conditions for most of the year. Both plants do well in large pots with good quality, freely draining potting mix that is kept damp. They fare best in summer temperatures of 18–28°C with plenty of bright light, including a few hours of direct sun each day. Their pots can be moved outdoors during the warmest months.

Where they differ is in their winter treatment: since *Strelitzia* come from the southern tip of South Africa, they actually experience a cool winter, when they should be kept at about 10–15°C with drier soil. *Heliconia*, conversely, are tropical and like to be warm and damp all year round, so they are best kept in a warm conservatory or greenhouse during winter.

Bird of Paradise & lobster claw flowers

PASSION FLOWERS

Beyond insects and birds, some plant species produce flowers that are pollinated exclusively (or nearly exclusively) by mammals, such as the Traveller's Palm of Madagascar, which is visited by lemurs. Many other plant species have flowers that attract bats or rodents, particularly at night.

Other plants evolved to attract a broad range of pollinators to maximise their chances of being fertilised successfully. Passion flowers (*Passiflora*) produce some of the most colourful and bizarre flowers in the entire plant kingdom. There are over 550 species of passion flowers, and they occur in almost every possible combination of colours, often with incredible stripes and patterns.

Most species come from Central and South America, and attract a wide range of pollinators, that can include not only bees, wasps and beetles, but bats and hummingbirds too!

HOW TO GROW

Most passion flowers require hot, steamy temperatures, but there is a surprising exception. The Blue Passion Flower (*Passiflora caerulea*) may look totally tropical, but it will grow outdoors all year round in the UK, tolerating frosts and temperatures as low as -10°C!

Ensure that your passionflower has moist, rich, well-drained garden or potting soil. Grow it either in a flowerbed against a trellis or wall where it can climb, or in a pot of 30cm diameter or more with a climbing support. It doesn't need special watering or any other care. This mostly evergreen plant will thrive in full sun and within one year can produce hundreds of flowers a season, especially if given good quality fertilizer to promote flowering. It's good that so many new flowers keep appearing, as these ornate blooms stay open for just one day.

If you succeed in growing the Blue Passion Flower, you can try some of the more exotic (non-hardy) species in a warm conservatory or on a sunny windowsill.

Passion flowers 67

THE COLOUR OF FLOWERS

Plants produce flowers in a wide rainbow of colours. The colour of each flower is not random, but specially evolved to enable each plant species to attract a specific pollinator.

The eyesight of birds is particularly well attuned to the red end of the light spectrum, so many large red flowers are adapted to attract bird visitors. Since most birds do not have a sense of smell, most bird-pollinated flowers are scentless to prevent the plant from spending energy on producing scents that would otherwise be wasted.

Compared to most birds, the eyes of insects pollinators are adapted to sense a wider range of colours, including ultraviolet light (which our human eyes cannot detect). Flowers adapted to insect pollinators often arise in a broader range of colours, but also often have patterns that we (humans) cannot see. Those 'secret' patterns which are visible only to insects are created by the flower either reflecting or absorbing ultraviolet light.

68 Unbelievable flowers

Bright blue flowers are relatively uncommon in nature. However, in Tibet, there is a uniquely high concentration of blue-flowered plants, with over 80 species that have bright blue petals or other flower parts. Several species of *Meconopsis* poppies (left) have stunning electric blue blooms. No one knows exactly why Tibet should hold such a concentration of plant species with blue flowers. Some botanists believe that at high altitudes, where ultraviolet light levels are very high, blue flowers may work better than other colours in attracting insect pollinators.

Black flowers are even rarer than blue ones because black, as a colour, absorbs light rather than reflects it, so often is not very conspicuous. Plants that do produce black flowers often have bright yellow reproductive parts that are made extremely visible by the contrast with their darker surroundings, emphasising where pollinators should go. While there are very few naturally occurring wild black flowers, horticulturists have bred a wide range of plants in cultivation with stunning dark petals. Among the most common are black-flowered pansies (below) that are popular in gardens across the world!

ULTRAVIOLET VISION!

It is well known amongst biologists that insects do not see the same spectra of light that humans do. This is certainly true of bees, beetles and butterflies, which are important pollinators of plants. Scientists have shown that if you view a flower like our insect friends do, they look completely different. It has been suggested that the UV-dark areas in the middle of flowers are used by insects to navigate to valuable nectar and pollen sources. Pollen itself often glows brightly under UV light, allowing insects that feed on it to home in on the centre of the flowers!

The colour of flowers

World's SMELLIEST flowers

Not all plants are sweet-smelling roses or fragrant pansies. Many plants stink. Some smell of rotting meat. Others stench of dung. A few smell like rancid fish! The world's smelliest flowers can be so pongy, that you can smell some from 20 metres away or more.

There are many stinky plants that you can grow at home to amaze and startle your friends, parents and neighbours!

WHAT DO SMELLY FLOWERS LOOK LIKE?

Flowers designed to entice pollinators attracted to rotting meat often share similar traits. Rather then being brightly coloured, flowers are often shades of orange, brown, red or purple in order to mimic flesh. To add to the illusion, they often have rough or warty surfaces, and coverings of hair. Many of the world's smelliest flowers are short-lived, releasing a concentrated stink over just a few days.

WHY DO SOME FLOWERS STINK?

While most flowers produce sweet-smelling nectar to attract bees and butterflies, a few have specialised to attract pollinators that like rotting meat and dung, such as carrion flies and blow flies. So, in order to attract those pollinators effectively, flowers with revolting smells and unusual appearances are needed!

The well-named skunk cabbage!

Where do the SMELLIEST flowers and fruit come from?

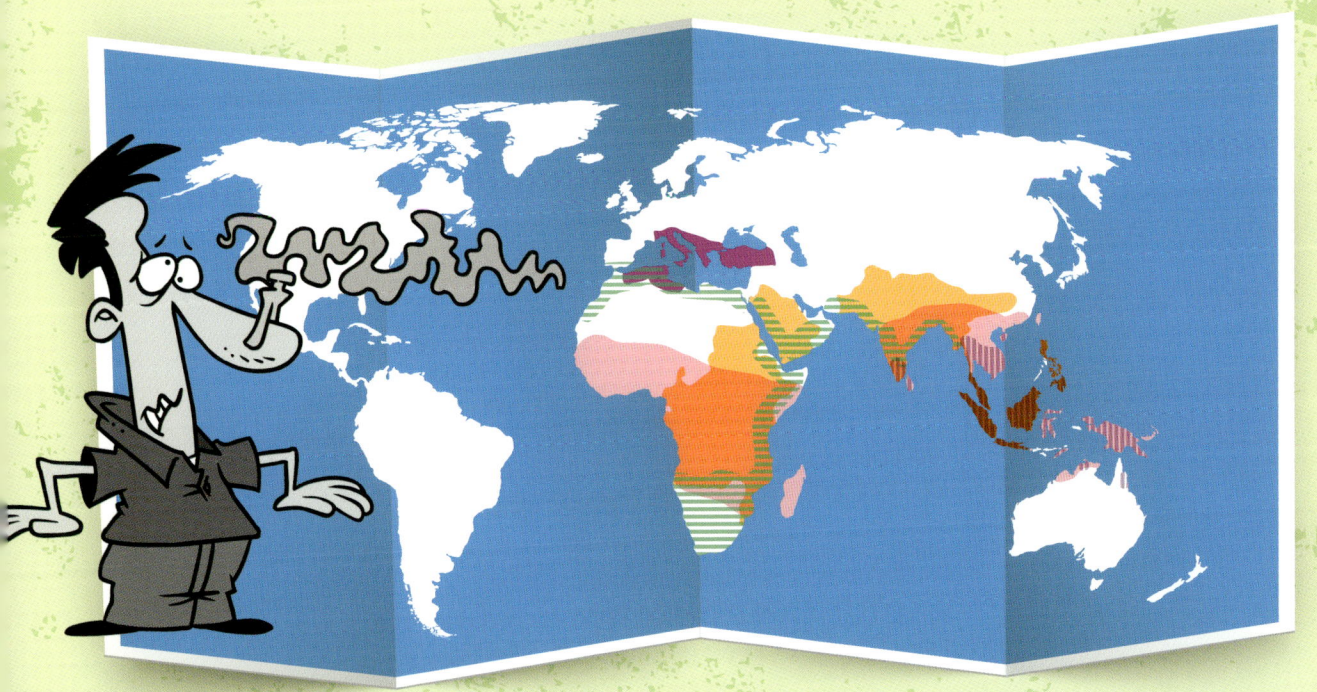

- Amorphophalus
- Typhonium venosum
- Dracunculus
- Stapelidae
- Rafflesia
- Durian

There are hundreds of types of disgusting-smelling plants found across the world – certainly too many to cram into this one book. These plants are found in all sorts of environments, and include the bizarrely beautiful (and rank!) starfish flowers, found across Africa and the Middle East, the stinking giant arums from parts of Asia, Africa, Australia and nearby islands, the colourful and putrid Dragon Lilies from the Mediterranean region, the durian fruit from Southeast Asia, and the furiously unpleasant Voodoo Lily, from Africa and Asia.

Luckily, some of the most smelly of the smelly plants are also some of the most spectacular, including giant flowers, murderous flowers and fruits that reek of garbage. What's not to love?

Smelly Feet Tree

Some of the world's smelliest plants are totally bizarre. Believe it or not, there is a bushy shrub from Mexico that is called the Sweaty Feet Plant (*Deherainia smaragdina*). It produces small green flowers (because it attracts pollinators not by sight, but by smell), and its petals stink with a cheesy and sweaty odour!

PARASITIC FLOWERS

The genus *Rafflesia* is even weirder! *Rafflesia* are parasitic plants from Asia that live inside a host vine. There are approximately 28 species, none of which produce leaves or any other visible parts except flowers and fruit. They live as a network of fibre-like tissues within their host vine, and steal all the energy they need to produce gigantic flowers. The largest *Rafflesia* species of all produces a warty, orange flower up to 1 metre across (see page 48), which is the largest single flower on Earth! Each *Rafflesia* flower lives for only a few days (usually less than six), and when they first open, they release quite a smell to attract a range of carrion-loving insects.

Rafflesia pricei

DEADLY DECEPTOR PLANTS!

The group of Asian plants called *Rhizanthes* is closely related to *Rafflesia* but produce perhaps even more grotesque flowers. *Rhizanthes* blooms look like an exploded octopus spread on the ground. They have many petals, each of which terminate in a tendril that spreads onto the rainforest floor. *Rhizanthes* also stinks of rotting meat and attracts carrion flies to its smelly, brownish, hairy blooms. The deception is so perfect that the flies often lay eggs on the surface of the bloom (thinking it to be a dead animal). As they explore the flower, the pollen-laden flies fertilise the bloom. The fly eggs frequently hatch, and tiny maggots crawl over the surface of the *Rhizanthes* flower, only to find no meat meal at all. The maggots eventually all die of starvation or are killed by ants which climb onto the flower by crawling along the strange tentacles. For this reason, one *Rhizanthes* species is called *Rhizanthes infanticida* – the infant (baby fly) killing plant!

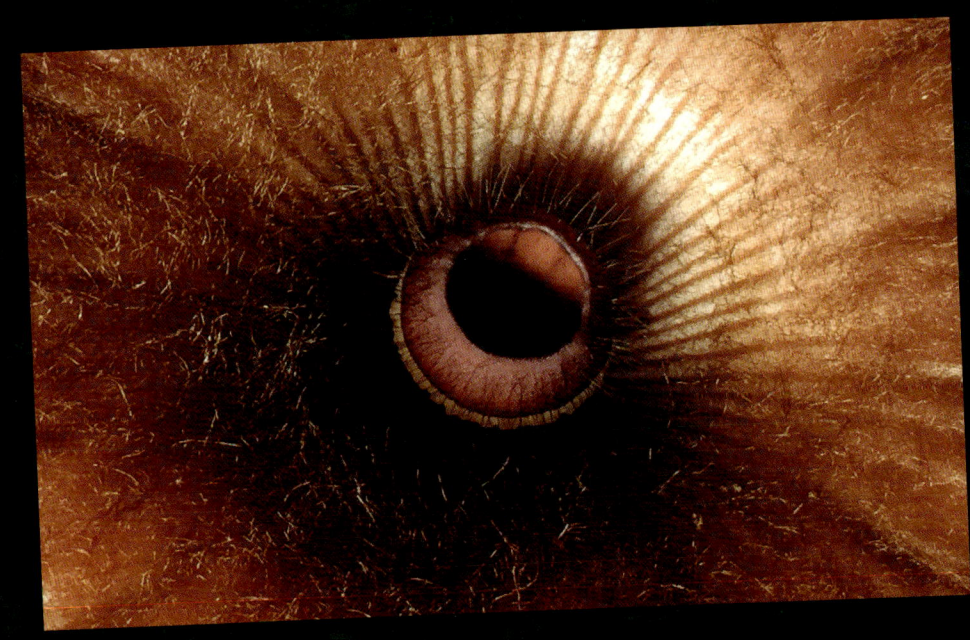

74 World's smelliest flowers

Stinky KING OF FRUIT

Its not just flowers that stink. Some fruit also use horrible smells to attract animals to eat their flesh and distribute their seeds. One of the world's smelliest fruit is called the durian (*Durio zibethinus*). Originating in South-east Asia, the durian looks like a spiky football. It can weigh several kilograms and hangs from a tree. Inside the fruit, large seeds are covered with a yellow or cream-coloured paste. The rind of the fruit and the paste have a strong odour that is often likened to rotten onions or raw sewage! People usually either hate the stink of the fruit, or adore it. In many parts of Asia, this smelly fruit is regarded as a delicacy, with a taste that is savoury, sweet and creamy all at once and it is often called the King of Fruits!

Deceptive plants & stinky fruit

Starfish Flowers
(Stapelia and relatives)

This family of dwarf succulents includes several genera, of which *Stapelia*, *Edithcolea*, *Huernia* and *Orbea* are the best known and most widely grown. These plants are called starfish flowers because their five-lobed blooms look like starfish. They are also sometimes called carrion flowers, because they stink of rotting meat to attract pollinators.

Starfish flower plants produce low-growing, fleshy, grey-green leafless stems that often turn bright orange or red when exposed to direct sunlight. The stems may be up to 25cm high, are often four-sided and sometimes hairy. While starfish flowers might look like cacti, these stinky but spectacular plants actually belong to a completely different group of succulents.

Where do they come from?

Starfish flowers come from the deserts and dry plains of Africa, particularly South Africa and neighbouring countries.

How does it grow?

In their desert habitats, starfish flowers are exposed to extreme conditions, including intense sunlight, high temperatures and very little rain. They often grow amongst rocks or under other plants where they receive a little protection from the searing conditions. Their short stems creep and scramble over the ground, spreading into large patches where the conditions are ideal.

Starfish flower plants' thick, fleshy leaves store water very effectively, and they may survive for months without receiving any water at all! The stems tend to break into segments as the plant gets older, and the pieces fall away to root where they land, enabling the plant to spread.

Flowers

While many species of starfish flower produce blooms that are 5 or 6cm across, the biggest of all (*Stapelia gigantea*) produces flowers that can be up to 41cm in diameter when fully open!

The blooms of starfish flowers are five-lobed, flat and often have dramatic and intricate banded or spotted patterns of red, purple, yellow, orange and black. The delicate reproductive parts are in the middle of the flower, often arranged in a star shape.

Starfish flowers 77

The striking colours and patterns make the flowers contrast with the otherwise uniform desert landscape, so they stand out to attract pollinating insects. Amazingly, the flowers are even more brightly coloured than we can see! Many starfish flowers have patterns viewed only in ultraviolet light, which we humans cannot see, but which make the flowers even more eye-catching to pollinating insects which can.

The flowers also mimic the body of a dead animal. Many species have petals that are covered in hairs with uneven surfaces to mimic decaying animal matter. Some starfish flowers have a hole in the centre of the bloom to resemble a natural opening or wound. In some species, each flower may open for only a few days; in others, the blooms may last for a week or more.

The deception is very effective. Flies are fooled into laying their eggs on the flowers thinking the petals are rotting meat. While they look for the best place to lay their eggs, they inadvertently pollinate the blooms. Often, the fly eggs hatch out into tiny maggots that quickly die of starvation.

78 World's smelliest flowers

What does it SMELL like?

Starfish flowers really stink! In many species, the smell is a putrid odour of rotting carrion that attracts blow flies. Sometimes people describe the stench as resembling rancid fish, rotting meat or poo!

Flowers are usually particularly smelly on hot afternoons, and the scent can be carried for many metres.

If you want to surprise your parents or neighbours with a really terrible smell, this is the perfect plant to grow!

Starfish flowers 79

HOW TO GROW

Many starfish flowers are really easy to grow and are extremely low maintenance. The species *Stapelia variegata* is one of the easiest, has really interesting flowers and is recommended for the beginner.

You can grow starfish flowers from seed, but it takes at least three years for seedlings to reach flowering size. So to experience a smelly flower more quickly, buy either established plants or rooted cuttings.

Since starfish flowers are desert plants that grow in sandy, fast draining, rocky locations, they need a gritty soil. A blend of one part potting soil and four parts sand or grit works well. Choose a pot that drains well (with several holes at the bottom), preferably one that is unglazed and will allow evaporation of excess moisture. The pot should be just big enough to hold the starfish plant securely. Many species actually prefer a slightly crowded environment and this also keeps the plant tight and compact.

You can grow starfish flowers year-round on a sunny windowsill or in a conservatory, or during the summer in a greenhouse or outside as a patio plant. They are not tolerant of cold weather, and will die if exposed to freezing conditions. If you grow starfish flowers outdoors, it is best to move them inside when temperatures drop to below 10°C.

Too much sun causes the stems to develop protective reddish or purple pigmentation and can eventually slow growth. Too little light leads to weak, thin growth with decreased flower production. During winter, falling temperatures and reduced light levels trigger starfish flowers to become dormant or grow very slowly.

Be very careful not to overwater your starfish flower. As with most succulents, they are prone to rot if kept too wet and this is the most frequent cause of death in cultivation. In winter, starfish flowers need hardly any water at all and should be watered just once every month. In spring and through summer, water when the soil is dry to the touch (normally once every week or two). If in doubt, don't water your starfish flower. If conditions are too dry, the stems will wrinkle. After watering, the stems will return to their normal shape.

World's smelliest flowers

To minimise the chance of rotting, many growers find it best to place the pot in a saucer of water for an hour to allow the soil to absorb water, rather than watering from above. Between watering times, make sure the pot can drain freely. Standing a starfish flowerpot permanently in a saucer of water will cause root rot.

You will rarely need to repot your starfish flower, although you should change the soil every two years.

Given a warm, sunny position, your starfish flower will produce its spectacular flower.

To encourage more frequent flowering, apply fertiliser at half the recommended strength every two weeks during spring and summer. Stop fertilising your plant in late August to prevent new growth from forming while the plant goes into dormancy.

It is very easy to multiply starfish flowers by taking cuttings. Simply detach one or more of your plant's stems and place them in a shady, dry area for three days to allow the cut surface of the cutting to seal and form a callus. Then lie the cuttings on top of a pot of starfish flower soil (rather than planting them, which makes them far more prone to rot). Within three months, roots should form. During the first summer season, water the cuttings once a week, then treat as adult starfish flower plants thereafter.

You can have no end of fun showing people the exotic-looking flowers, asking them to smell them and then watching their faces.

ARUMS

The arum family (Araceae), also often known as aroids, are a diverse and fascinating group of plants from across temperate, subtropical and tropical regions of the world. All aroids have a distinctive and unusual flower structure. Many small flowers are packed tightly together around the base of a club-like spadix, which is in turn surrounded by a hooded spathe. The shape, size and colour of the spadix and spathe varies enormously between different arum species.

Although arums are often called 'arum lilies', they are not members of the true lily family.

DRAGON LILY
(Dracunculus vulgaris)

Also know as Dragonwort and the Dragon Arum, this plant has many names which refer to the ferocious appearance of the flowers. It is occasionally also referred to as stink lily owing to the mighty pong that the flowers produce.

Where does it come from?

The Dragon Lily grows across the Eastern Mediterranean region, namely Greece, Crete, the Aegean Islands, the Balkans and parts of south-west Turkey.

It is found in a variety of habitats, including woodland, scrub and waste land and even in roadsides.

How does it grow?

Early in spring, each Dragon Lily plant grows as a bud that emerges out of the ground like a dragon's snout. After a few weeks of growing, the bud enlarges and unfurls to reveal jagged leaves that stand up to 1m tall and often have beautiful patterns and spots somewhat like dragon scales (see opposite page).

After several leaves are produced, each adult plant produces a wicked-looking flower. The flowers are followed by green berries which ripen to a stunning orange-red. The plant then dies down to become dormant over winter.

Flowers

The flowers of the Dragon Lily are bewitchingly beautiful and sinister. They have a deep purple, velvety tongue-like spathe and a large, black, horn-like spadix. As soon as the flowers open, they release a terrible stench which is described as a dragon's breath! Each flower may stand up to 70cm tall, and be up to 45cm long. It opens for just a few days before it withers.

What does it SMELL like?

The Dragon Lily really stinks. The smell is released on the first day of flowering, then reduces as the bloom ages. Most people describe the stink this flower creates as reminiscent of rotting meat or road kill.

HOW TO GROW

This plant is really easy to grow as a garden plant in the UK. It is best to buy a large plant during spring or summer and plant it in a sunny or lightly shaded area in your garden in humus-rich, well drained soil.

Water every three days during summer to ensure the soil is moist. It is a good idea to give the Dragon Lily slow-release fertiliser and to apply a general fertiliser solution at half the recommended strength once every month during the growing season. This will encourage the production of a flower during the following spring.

During winter months, it can be left alone and is hardy across the UK.

Be warned though. The Dragon Lily can be very smelly. Its fragrance can waft over many metres (so if you plant your Dragon Lily near your parents' window, they may not be impressed). The smell can attract masses of flies too. So you may need to think carefully about which part of the garden that you grow it to best revel in the awe and disgust that this plant brings!

Dragon Lily 85

GIANT ARUMS
(Amorphophallus)

The giant arum family comprises over 200 species, including several species that produce truly gigantic flowers (see the Titan Arum in the Unbelievable Flowers chapter, page 50).

Many of the giant arums produce really bizarre flowers that often have a massive spadix.

Where does it come from?

Giant arum plants come from tropical and subtropical parts of Asia, Africa, Australia and nearby islands. Many species grow in forests, often in shade.

How does it grow?

In most giant arum species, each plant produces just one leaf each year. The leaf emerges from an underground tuber, called a corm. The corm (right) can be enormous (in some species weighing over 100kg). It stores the nutrients and starch reserves that the plant requires for both flowering and growing leaves.

Giant arums 87

Giant arum leaves are shaped like palm trees, usually with a beautifully mottled stem. Each leaf stays alive for several months, then withers. The plant then produces a new leaf and the cycle is repeated, one giant leaf at a time.

Every new leaf adds more and more nutrients and starch to the underground corm until eventually the plant is ready to produce a single, spectacular bloom!

The leaves of the biggest species of giant arums can be the size of a small tree!

After flowering, a spike bearing berries is produced, each containing a single seed. The seeds are dispersed by animals that eat the berries. After the berries are ripe, each giant arum plant usually becomes dormant for a few months, before beginning the production of leaves once more.

The Elephant Foot Yam (*Amorphophallus paeoniifolius*) is eaten widely across Southeast Asia

Flowers

Giant arum flowers are among the most spectacular of all blooms. Each species has a different flower shape, size and colour, but in many, the spathe is shaped like an upturned funnel, out of which a giant spadix towers to act like a chimney to disperse the bloom's powerful (often revolting) scent!

As the flowers of giant arums can be enormous, these must rank among the stinkiest of all plants! Each flower typically dies after just three to five days.

What does it SMELL like?

The flowers of giant arums have a distinctive scent of decay. Different species have different smells, but most wreak of rotting meat or fish!

Giant arums

A SMELLY RAINFOREST CHIMNEY

Many of the biggest giant arums grow in the rainforests of Borneo and Sumatra. Several species produce gigantic flowers that are more than 2m tall! In these titanic blooms, the spadix works like a chimney and spreads the scent efficiently in even the faintest of jungle breezes. In some species, the spadix actually heats up to disperse the smell more effectively. This is a major advance over other flowers that use colour to attract pollinators, since insects can be attracted to the flower even if they cannot see it in the dense rainforest vegetation! Since each giant arum plant flowers so infrequently, the nearest open bloom may be many kilometres away, so it is essential that the plant attracts pollinators from as far away as possible!

World's smelliest flowers

HOW TO GROW

Giant arums (*Amorphophallus*) range in size from the world's largest unbranched flower scape (see page 50) to surprisingly small species just 10–15cm tall. However, most species are between 30cm and 150cm in height, and come in many shapes and sizes. The best plants for a beginner to try are Devil's Tongue *Amorphophallus konjac* (right), *A. paeoniifolius* and *A. bulbifer* (left). All three of these can be purchased from many nurseries, and each one has a very different flower to the other.

In growth, *Amorphophallus* invariably do well in a large pot of rich, free-draining, good-quality potting soil. Plants should be kept moist and warm when in growth, generally at 20–30°C, in bright shade with some sun, plus occasional fertiliser given to help them produce a large corm during the growing season. In winter, their single leaf will die back, and the soil should be kept almost dry to prevent rot. Some people even dig up the corms to store them cool and dry until new growth starts to appear. After a few good seasons, the plants will produce their huge flowers in place of a leaf, letting you know you did everything right.

If you are really keen, the largest species, *Amorphophallus titanum*, can be grown, but it is not a beginner's plant, requiring hot year-round temperatures, careful winter care and a huge amount of space!

Amorphophallus bulbifer

Devil's Tongue *Amorphophallus konjac*

Giant arums 91

The giant arum Devil's Tongue (page 91) has a smelly little cousin called the Voodoo Lily that is also great fun to grow!

VOODOO LILY
(Typhonium venosum)

Although it comes from temperate and tropical Africa and Asia, the Voodoo Lily is more cold tolerant than the Devil's Tongue, and when planted in well drained soil, it can survive outdoors throughout the winter in most parts of the UK. For best results, unearth the corms and store them in the same ways as recommended for the Devil's Tongue (see page 91).

The Voodoo Lily is so called because it can flower without being planted in soil and before receiving any water (as if through magic or sorcery). Large Voodoo Lily corms can produce flowers up to 60cm tall, but in this species, the flower is very narrow (usually just a few centimetres across). The inside of the spathe is patterned in a really weird mix of rich maroon and yellow blotches. The outside of the spadix can be purple, brown or green.

The spadix is often massive in proportion to the flower. It is thin, tapers to a point and is dark red, brown or black, like a weird, wiry alien antenna.

World's smelliest flowers

The whole flower emits a foul odour much like that of the giant arums, although in this species, it is often described as smelling like cow manure!

After flowering, the Voodoo Lily usually produces two exotic-looking leaves during the growing season, although occasionally a third can appear. The corms of this species can weigh up to 2kg, but are usually smaller. Offset corms are often produced, allowing easy propagation of further Voodoo Lilies.

HOW TO GROW

The Voodoo Lily certainly looks like a tropical exotic, but in the wild it can be found at elevations of up to 3,900m. This is good news for growers from cold countries, as it tolerates hard freezes when dormant.

This species is most commonly purchased as a dormant corm, but occasionally as seed. The corm should be planted 10–15cm deep in a rich, loam-based potting compost at the first evidence of new growth. It can be grown in a 20cm pot or even in a garden bed if it's raised to ensure that its soil is able to drain freely. During the growing season, temperatures of 15–25°C are ideal, and during growth the soil should be kept damp. As winter approaches, the leaf will die back. At this point, some growers lift the corm to protect it from winter wet, or move the pot to a dry sheltered spot.

A mature corm may produce a flower in the late winter well before the leaves or roots emerge. The plant doesn't actually need to be potted at this stage and can be presented as it is, as a curiosity for friends and family to gawk at. However, as soon as the roots and leaves begin to appear, transfer it to a pot and begin watering!

Funky fruit & veg

We all know that fruit and vegetables are good for us, though perhaps not always exciting, so how about adding some downright weird and wonderful characters into the mix!

All of the crop plants which produce the fruit and vegetables that people eat today were originally developed from wild plants, in some cases thousands of years ago.

As civilisations around the world emerged, the first farmers in each area found different groups of edible plants in their local area that they could cultivate to produce delicious vegetables and fruits. Wild plants were selectively bred to create bigger and tastier fruit, in ever greater amounts. Gradually, this process produced the fruit and vegetables that we know today.

Of course, each region of the world has very different groups of native plants, and the different civilisations came to rely on different crops as their fruit and vegetable staples.

Today, we have access to fruit and vegetables from all corners of the globe, but the types of fruits and vegetables that you see in the supermarket are just a few of the tens of thousands of crop plants that humans have developed across the world over thousands of years. Many of the fruits and vegetables that we know today are actually just popular examples of really diverse fruits and vegetables that actually occur in amazing ranges of colours, shapes and sizes in the regions where they were originally cultivated.

For example, beans aren't just baked, broad or green. There are thousands of types of beans in all shapes, sizes and colours.

Many parts of the world have completely different fruits and vegetables to those we are familiar with. The apples and pears we eat here every day, are their exotic and expensive rarities! For example, in many parts of tropical Indonesia, temperate fruits can be difficult to find, but bright red bananas and the bizarre-looking snake fruit (a fruit of a palm with scaly brown skin) are the everyday.

Here are some of the strangest and most delicious fruits and vegetables which you can grow at home to surprise your family and brighten up your dinner.

RAINBOW CARROTS

PURPLE CARROTS

Carrots are the roots of the wild carrot, *Daucus carota*, a species thought to have originated in the mountains of Afghanistan and Iran, long since domesticated across Asia and Europe.

Purple carrots, for example, come from the Middle East and Turkey and are rich in anthocyanins which are known to guard against heart disease. Red carrots originate from China and India.

We think of carrots as bright orange, skinny tap roots, but the orange carrots we know today were actually bred by Dutch growers during the 16th and 17th centuries. Before then, carrots occurred in a rainbow of colours, including purple, red, white and yellow, and in a variety of shapes, from small, ball-shaped ones to wide, chunky ones! Most of these unusual varieties of carrots are very easy to grow. So why not give it a go!

Funky fruit & veg

RECOMMENDED VARIETIES

There are hundreds of varieties of carrots from across the world. The following are among the most colourful and vigorous:

'Purple Haze' & 'Purple Dragon'

These varieties of carrots have deep-purple coloured skin and flesh.

'Cosmic Purple'

This variety has purple skin and outer flesh, and bright orange inner flesh. Looks out of this world sliced.

'Yellowstone' & 'Solar Yellow'

Both of these varieties have bright yellow skin and flesh.

'White Satin' & 'Belgium White'

Pure white carrots.

'Red Samurai' & 'Atomic Red'

These two varieties have blood-red skin and flesh.

HOW TO GROW

Carrots are among the easiest vegetables to grow in your garden, and you can get full-sized carrots within as few as 70 days from germination!

For best results, carrots should be planted in loose, sandy soil free of large stones (unless you want to have fun growing misshapen forms), in a sunny or lightly shaded area. It's a good idea to grow them in a raised bed or with a 60cm (or more) high fleece fence around them to guard against the carrot fly, which only flies low to the ground. Rake an area of suitable soil so that it is free of weeds and other plants, and sow carrot seeds in rows 20cm apart, in groups of five seeds, spaced 4cm apart.

Carrots like cool temperatures and grow best in spring and autumn. You can start sowing the seeds three weeks before the last expected frost. Ensure that the soil remains moist, but not wet. The seeds should start to grow in one to three weeks after planting. Plan ahead, as the latest you can plant carrot seeds is around three months before the first expected frost of winter.

Gently remove excess carrot seedlings, as crowded carrot plants will produce smaller, crooked carrots! Remove the weaker seedlings by pulling them out of the ground so that you are left with individual plants growing in rows.

Water your carrot plants if the weather is dry, or they may split underground. After 70 days of growth, check the size of your carrots by gently removing a little soil from the top of the root.

The flavour of carrots is best when they are freshly harvested. Gently pull the foliage at the tops of the carrot roots, or use a garden fork or trowel to loosen the soil and lift the roots without breaking them. Watering your carrot bed before harvesting can soften the soil and make pulling easier.

WHITE STRAWBERRIES!

Strawberries are delicious, but there is a little-known relative called the pineberry which is perhaps even tastier! It is so-called because it tastes just like pineapple and produces little white berries (up to 2cm across) that are speckled with red seeds (the opposite of normal strawberries).

Pineberries are actually hybrid strawberries involving species from Europe, North America and Chile, so they do not occur naturally. Pineberries do not grow true from seed, so you will need to buy young starter plants to grow true pineberries successfully.

RECOMMENDED VARIETIES

'Natural Albino', 'White Carolina' & 'White D'

These are among the best pineberry varieties available.

HOW TO GROW

Pineberries are great fun to grow, and they can be cultivated by the same method as strawberry plants:

Pineberry plants can be grown in rows in your garden, or in window boxes, patio pots or hanging baskets. Many garden centres now sell special strawberry pots with holes in their sides. These are great, as both strawberry and pineberry plants have trailing fruit that will cascade over the side of the pot.

For best results, plant your pineberry plants as early in the year as possible after the last frosts of spring, and as soon as starter plants are available.

Select a sunny location where the plants will be exposed to at least half a day of direct sunlight. The soil should be well drained to prevent root and crown rot. Mix garden compost or composted manure into the soil, and add a slow-release organic fertiliser (according to directions on the packet) to encourage vigorous growth. If you are planting pineberry plants in your garden, rake an area so that it is weed free.

When planting pineberries, take care that the soil is not higher than the top of the crown (that is the stem and the leaves). Pack soil gently but firmly around the roots. Position your plants 15cm apart as growth will be stunted if the plants are too crowded.

Water your plants well two or three times a week, but not every day. Make sure that the soil remains moist but not waterlogged, and throughout the growing season, make sure that the growing area is frequently cleared of weeds.

After a month or two, delicate white flowers will be produced. Some varieties of pineberry will only produce fruit if they are grown with other varieties that act as pollinator plants. Check this with the supplier when you buy your starter plants. If successfully pollinated, your plants will produce fruit throughout summer, sometimes as soon as two months after planting!

Just as with strawberry plants, pineberries naturally form runners that sprout roots and eventually grow independently. You can carefully separate the runners from the mother plant, and pot then up as daughter plants.

Watering should be reduced during autumn, and no watering will be needed during winter. Most pineberry varieties can be left outside during winter in the UK, provided they are covered with a layer of straw mulch. Potted plants can brought into a cool greenhouse, conservatory, garage or cellar to overwinter.

White strawberries

BLACK TOMATOES

Believe it or not, tomatoes actually belong to the nightshade family, which includes many very poisonous relatives! The fruit of wild tomato species often have very bitter tastes, but some are sweeter than others. They originate in the Andes of South America, and it is thought that the first tomatoes arrived in Europe from Peru, having been transported home by the Spanish. One of the earliest names given to tomatoes in Italy meant 'golden apple', as the earliest cultivated varieties were actually yellow, not red! You can try growing yellow, orange and pink tomatoes too.

RECOMMENDED VARIETIES

Literally thousands of varieties of tomatoes have been bred. The most interesting are varieties that develop fruit of deep black (but otherwise taste the same) and gigantic 'beefsteak' tomatoes that can weigh several kilos! Some of the best varieties are:

'Black Beauty'

One of the darkest varieties of tomatoes that exists. Develops purplish-black skins with dark red flesh, and has medium-sized fruit.

'Black Cherry'

A really small, dark-skinned tomato that develops dark purplish skin and red flesh. Each plant produces an abundance of small fruit.

'Black Prince', 'Black Krim', 'Black Brandywine' & 'Cherokee'

Dark blackish-red on the outside, often bright red on the inside.

'Gigantomo'

('Steakhouse' in the USA) is the biggest of all beefsteak tomatoes, producing fruit of about 1.3kg, but the current world record weighed in at 3.51kg!

100 Funky fruit & veg

HOW TO GROW

Tomatoes are easy to grow and can yield a lot of fruit.

The plants prefer direct sunlight, especially black-fruited varieties which need high light levels to develop their dark colour – generally, the more exposed to the sun they are, the blacker the tomatoes will be.

For best results, grow your tomato plants in a large pot of soil or in a tomato grow bag ('grobag') in an unheated greenhouse or conservatory.

Tomato plants can also be successfully cultivated outside in a sunny, sheltered position in patio pots, window boxes or in rows in vegetable patches.

They should always be positioned at least 45cm apart, as each plant needs sufficient light and space to grow. The soil should be well drained and, for best results, mix in garden compost and add a slow-release organic fertiliser to encourage vigorous growth.

If growing from seed, sow in the greenhouse during February to April, or outdoors during March and April. Germination will take place in one to two weeks. You may find it faster and easier to buy starter plants in spring.

Keep the young tomato plants well watered, especially during dry weather. The soil must be kept moist but not waterlogged.

Your tomato plants will grow quickly. Remove dead leaves as your plants grow. Each plant will grow between 1 and 2m tall, and will need support from an early age in order for the stem to grow upright. The easiest method is to use canes, tying the plant's stem to the cane at regular intervals.

As your tomato plant grows, it will produce many side shoots at the leaf joints. It is best that these are pinched out and removed to prevent your plant from becoming too bushy.

One to two months after germination, small yellow flowers will be produced and, if pollinated, small green tomatoes will start to develop and enlarge. Apply liquid fertiliser only when your plant has several small tomatoes that are starting to swell (as feeding the plant earlier will discourage flower production).

The fruit should be allowed to fully ripen on the plant before being picked. The first fruit will be ready to harvest two to three months after flowering. Really large, beefsteak tomatoes will require longer for the fruit to reach full size. To encourage huge fruit, allow each beefsteak tomato plant to produce just one fruit by removing all others.

PURPLE POTATOES

Originally from South America, potato plants have been cultivated for at least 5,000 years (some believe for as long as 8,000) The potato plant belongs to the same family as the tomato, so it is also related to many very poisonous plant species, yet its cultivation became essential to indigenous communities across Peru, Bolivia and much of the Andes. During the last 500 years, the humble potato has been carried across the world and become the staple crop for hundreds of millions of people.

The large, pale tubers we know as potatoes are just a few of thousands of types of potatoes still grown in South America. Across the Andes, potato tubers can be found in a startling spectrum of colours, from bright yellow to red, maroon, purple, black and white. They also vary in shape and size. Many varieties of potato have tiny, round tubers, others have knobbly ones shaped like pine cones, and yet others have long, pencil-shaped tubers (known as fingerling potatoes). The colour of the potato does not affect the flavour.

102 Funky fruit & veg

PURPLE CHIPS!

Many varieties of potatoes have deep-blue-coloured skins and flesh. These purple potatoes generally keep their unusual colour when they are cooked, and so can be used to make bright purple chips!

Purple potatoes

RECOMMENDED VARIETIES

Among the rainbow of potato varieties, the following stand out:

'Shetland Black'

A dark purple-skinned potato with white flesh that was developed during the Victorian Era on the Shetland Island. Legend has it that 'Shetland Black' potatoes came to the British Isles by way of a stranded Spanish Armada ship.

'Purple Majesty', 'Sapphire', 'Dragon Egg' & 'Adirondack Blue'

All of these varieties produce small or medium-sized potatoes that have dark skins and deep purple flesh. Purple Majesty is possibly the darkest purple variety of all.

'Purple Pelisse'

This variety produces small, narrow potatoes that have deep purple (almost black) skins, and purple flesh. The plants of this variety are smaller and more compact than many other purple potato strains.

'Duke of York', 'Kerr's Pink' & 'Red Rose'

These varieties produce potatoes that have red or pink skins, and light yellow flesh inside. They produce medium to large-sized potatoes and are very prolific.

'Cranberry Red'

This variety produces medium-sized potatoes that have bright red skin and pink flesh. Often the flesh is patterned with variable bands of pink and white.

'Austrian Crescent', 'Russian Banana' & 'Yukon Gold'

These varieties all produce medium to large potatoes with yellow skin and bright yellow flesh. These are very vigorous varieties and produce large crops.

Funky fruit & veg

HOW TO GROW

Potato plants prefer cool temperatures and should be grown outdoors in a vegetable patch in full sun with moist, rich soil. Soggy ground will cause potatoes to rot. Prepare the potato bed by turning the soil with a fork, then rake level and remove stones and clumps of weeds. If you don't have space for a potato bed, you can grow potatoes outdoors in a big bag or sack of soil-based compost.

It's best to buy 'seed potatoes' from potato breeders. Ordinary potatoes from the supermarket can be planted, but generally will not result in as large a yield of tubers.

Plant the seed potatoes directly into the potato bed in spring (if possible, before the last expected frost). Dig a hole 10cm deep for each seed potato, or a trench if you intend to plant many. Plant the whole seed potato (do not cut it up into smaller pieces). The eyes (little sprouts on the surface of the potato from which growth will emerge) should face upwards. Add compost or slow-release fertiliser around the tuber, cover it up with soil, and finally add a 10cm layer of mulch on top of the hole or trench.

Potato plants will emerge in four to six weeks. When each plant is around 10cm tall, gently pile up soil around each plant almost covering the foliage, but allow a few leaves to remain above the soil. This will ensure the potatoes remain below the level of the soil, and will promote tuber production.

Keep the soil moist so that the potato plants have sufficient water to produce potatoes, and ensure that the ground does not dry up during hot spells as uneven soil moisture levels will result in knobbly or cracked potatoes.

As soon as the plant starts to flower (usually about 10 weeks after planting), the potatoes are ready to be harvested. Each plant will have produced several potatoes underground along its root system. To harvest potatoes, gently excavate the top layer of soil using your hands or a trowel, while being careful not to disturb the rest of the plant. Gather some of the potatoes that have formed, and leave others undisturbed to continue to grow for harvesting throughout the growing season.

Please note: The leaves of potato plants are poisonous to humans and many animals, and should never be eaten.

JEWEL CORN

Sweetcorn, also known as maize, was domesticated in Central America from a species of grass around 9,000 years ago! It had been cultivated by indigenous people across the Americas for thousands of years, before it was encountered by European explorers and carried back to Europe some 500 years ago.

Sweetcorn remains the most widely grown crop across the Americas, where it is known as 'corn', and, particularly in Central America, it is eaten during almost every meal in one form or another. It has also become an important staple across many other parts of the world.

Funky fruit & veg

HOLY CORN!

Corn was more than a staple crop to many Central American cultures, not least the Aztecs, who worshipped several gods of corn, including Centeotl (the 'Corn Cob Lord'), Xilonen (goddess of sweetcorn) and Chicomecoátl (goddess of seed corn). Several figurines have been found with hairstyles resembling ears of corn, and Aztec mythology holds that the god Quetzalcoatl stole a kernel of corn to bring back to the humans to plant.

For at least 2,000 years, Black Aztec Corn has had a particularly important significance for indigenous groups of the Americas. It was (and still is) used to make an alcoholic drink called masato, and features in ancient folklore, ceremonial costumes and myths.

Jewel corn

RECOMMENDED VARIETIES

As with the potato, there are hundreds of ancient varieties of sweetcorn. Many have incredible colours, shapes and sizes!

'Black Aztec' sweetcorn

This beautiful black sweetcorn is known to have been grown by the ancient Aztecs as far back as 2,000 years ago and has been cultivated in Europe since the mid 19th century. It produces cobs with jet black kernels, but all other parts of 'Black Aztec' corn plants are the same as regular sweetcorn.

'Strawberry' sweetcorn

This variety produces really small, oval-shaped cobs (up to about 10cm long) with tiny, dark red or purple kernels that are great for making popcorn. This variety is often dried and its colourful cobs used for decoration.

'Oaxacan Green Dent' sweetcorn

A really unusual variety that produces green kernels, usually with cupped outer surfaces! 'Oaxacan Green Dent' sweetcorn is supposed to have been bred and cultivated by the Zapotec people, near Oaxaca, Mexico.

'Glass Gem' sweetcorn

A single cob may have kernels that are red, orange, yellow, white, bluish, pink, purple or green. The kernels have a particularly glossy outer layer, and resemble little jewels. It is often ground up into cornmeal to make tortillas or for making popcorn because it is very starchy.

'Bloody Butcher' sweetcorn

This variety of corn was introduced to settlers to Virginia in the 1840s by Native Americans. It produces cobs with variable red and purple kernels that reminded the settlers of the gory scenes of a butcher's slaughter house!

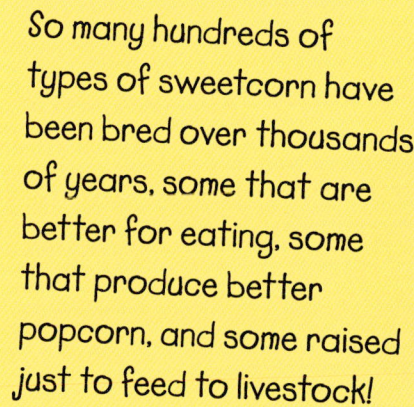

So many hundreds of types of sweetcorn have been bred over thousands of years, some that are better for eating, some that produce better popcorn, and some raised just to feed to livestock!

108 Funky fruit & veg

How to Grow

Sweetcorn can be successfully grown outdoors in the UK, and even the more exotic varieties from tropical regions of the Americas can produce ears of spectacularly coloured kernels if given a little care.

Many varieties of sweetcorn require temperatures of at least 15°C in order to germinate successfully, and need at least three months of warm temperatures in order to reach their full size (often up to 2m tall) and produce fully formed cobs.

Select an outdoor location offering direct or very strong sunlight in well-drained, nutrient-rich soil. For best results, mix compost or manure into the soil where sweetcorn plants will be planted, and apply a general-purpose nitrogen fertiliser before planting. Sweetcorn plants are wind pollinated and so should be planted in compact grids of short rows, rather than long, separate rows.

If conditions are suitably warm for germination, drop three seeds together in 3cm deep holes in the soil, 25cm apart from each other. Cover them with soil, and water thoroughly. If conditions outside are not warm enough, seed can be germinated in a terrarium, greenhouse or conservatory and planted outside after all risk of frost has passed.

Although many varieties of sweetcorn are drought tolerant, to achieve best results, the soil in which corn plants grow should remain moist, but not too wet, throughout the growing season. Keeping the soil moist is especially important as the plants flower and when the kernels are ripening.

Different varieties of sweetcorn should not be planted near one another, as cross-pollination generally produces poor-tasting, starchy corn.

Jewel corn | 09

Cucamelons

Also known as Mouse Melons or Mexican Sour Gherkins, cucamelons (*Melothria scabra*) are grape-sized members of the cucumber and melon family that taste of cucumber with a hint of lime, a flavour that becomes stronger as fruit are left to develop. They are one of the cutest-looking foods there is, making them very popular!

Cucamelons are native to Central America, and in Mexico are known as sandiitas de ratón, which means 'little mouse watermelons'. The fruits are only about 3cm long and are striped like watermelons, accounting for this common name. Although they are not commonly grown, they are becoming increasingly popular because they have a pleasant flavour, are adorable to look at, are easy to grow (and quite drought tolerant), and are mostly ignored by common plant pests.

Funky fruit & veg

At present, there are few varieties of this plant outside of Central America. While seeds are available through a few suppliers, the plants and fruit that they give rise to are all more or less similar, but no less exciting for that!

How to Grow

Cucamelons are frost tender, so they will die in winter. Therefore these fast-growing plants are best grown outdoors as annuals during the warmer months of the year, or in a warm conservatory year-round as a perennial pot plant.

Growing cucamelons is easy! It is best to sow the seeds indoors in March to April so that they are ready to move outside after the last spring frost. Seeds should be sown singly, with one placed in each 10cm diameter pot filled with good quality, freely draining potting soil. Cucamelons can take three to four weeks to germinate and may start off slowly, but will grow rapidly once their roots are established. In their natural habitat, they grow in full sun, so it is important that they get as much sunlight as possible.

Once conditions outside have warmed, they can be planted out. Dig holes of the same dimensions as your seedling pots about 30cm apart, transplant the seedlings, soil and all, to these holes and gently pat the soil in firmly around them. They should be watered immediately to help them settle, and periodically fertilised during the growing season to help them produce plentiful fruit. As they are strong climbers, it is useful to place a trellis or set of canes over the plants to prevent fruits trailing on the ground.

Water them once a week, or slightly more often in very hot and dry weather. After two or three months of growth, cucamelons will start to flower. It takes about two weeks after pollination for the fruit to become large enough to harvest. Ripe fruit are about the size of a grape, 3–4cm long, firm and plump. If left on the plants, the citrus-like flavour of the skin will intensify. The fruit can typically be picked from late July and continue through to October depending on the warmth of the growing season.

At the end of the growing season, potted cucamelons can be brought indoors to overwinter. The plants produce radish-like tubers that will survive the cold so long as they do not freeze. To prevent rot, simply stop watering until spring, when new growth emerges. Plants growing outside can be re-started from seed, or their tubers can be dug up and left in a pot of soil in a cool, dry place until the spring.

Cucamelons can be eaten fresh, used in salads, pickled, or even used to make summery drinks, just like cucumbers.

Cucamelons 111

SUPER-SHAPED WATERMELONS

Horticulturists in Japan have perfected the art of growing watermelons in moulds to shape the fruit into particular shapes. The most well known of the shaped watermelons are the cube-shaped ones, called 'square watermelons'. These oddities can fetch very high prices in Japan.

The rationale behind square watermelons is that they take up less room in the fridge and don't roll around. However, given how expensive they are, they remain a luxury item usually intended to show wealth, or maybe a strange sense of humour! In fact, some examples of square melons aren't even edible as they are not always fully developed when harvested. Ultimately, these fruit are a novelty decorative item that can truly surprise onlookers. Provided you can find a good quality mould, you can grow your own in your garden!

AMAZING APPLES

It is possible to grow almost any soft-fruit into unusual shapes using moulds. Apples work really well, although you will need a much smaller mould than that used for watermelons! Apple trees are very easy to grow and produce fruit even when grown as patio plants in tubs. Ask your parents or teachers if you can grow an apple tree at home or school to create your own super-shaped fruit.

SKULL FRUIT!

Watermelons have been grown into various shapes, including cubes, perfect spheres, hearts, and even skulls! Some have been grown to resemble statues of the Buddha! These shapes are created by placing developing fruit in moulds – it has nothing to do with genetics, only technique!

Super-shaped watermelons

YELLOW MELONS

There are over 1,200 varieties of watermelon that are grow commercially. Some have black rinds, others have flesh that is bright yellow! The yellow watermelons are a natural mutation and is known for its extremely sweet, honey-like taste. Other than its colour and flavour, yellow water melons are identical to the normal red varieties!

RECOMMENDED VARIETIES

Any typical variety of watermelon is suitable, but you should choose one that produces fruit of a size to suit the mould you have purchased or made.

HOW TO GROW

These plants are not difficult, but do need a long growing season and warm ground conditions to develop quickly. It is best to plant seeds in late winter indoors so that the seedlings can get a head start prior to planting out. Sow one to three seeds per pot in individual pots about 10cm in diameter, covering the seeds with about 3cm of good potting soil. Water them well and keep them at room temperature in a well-lit spot, a conservatory or bright window being ideal. Plants will usually emerge in a matter of two to three weeks and will rapidly increase in size. Consider removing all but the weakest plant in each pot. Once the last frost of the winter has passed, transfer the plants to their permanent positions in the garden. Watermelons are large, spreading plants, so each plant will require about one square metre.

The soil should be enriched with fertiliser and a rich compost mulch as these plants are heavy feeders. Feeding them will ensure that they develop quickly and produce large fruits. After one to two months of strong growth, the plants will flower.

Funky fruit & veg

Each watermelon plant can produce two to four large fruits per plant, and these require about 45–60 days to mature.

To produce a square watermelon, you need to place a transparent mould around a developing watermelon fruit. As the watermelon gets bigger, it gradually assumes the shape of the box. It is possible to buy moulds online, or to make your own. They should be slightly smaller than the average size of your mature watermelon variety and they must be strong, made of either tempered glass or thick, rigid plastic. Transparency ensures that the fruit receives plenty of sunlight and develops good coloration – otherwise the developing fruit will remain a sickly pale yellow colour. Provided all goes well, you will be able to harvest your square watermelon about one and a half months after your place it within its special mould.

HOW TO GROW

Super-shaped watermelons 115

DRAGON FRUIT

A PRETTY TOUGH CACTUS!

Dragon fruit are the large, striking and rather refreshing fruit of the *Hylocereus* cactus. They are cultivated in the tropics around the world, but particularly in Southeast Asia, the Caribbean and northern Australia. Their exact origins are uncertain, but the plants are native to Central America, occurring from Southern Mexico through Belize, Guatemala, El Salvador and Costa Rica. Two species of dragon fruit are commonly found, the white-fleshed *Hylocereus undatus*, and the red-fleshed *H. costaricensis*.

These extraordinary fruit are produced from striking, succulent stems that can become quite large. They evolved in the deserts and subtropical regions of Central America where, at least in winter, night-time temperatures can get very low. As a result, they can survive mild frosts through to heat waves of 40°C!

Funky fruit & veg

PRICKLY PEAR?

The dragon fruit isn't the only species of cactus to have edible fruits. In fact, lots of other species do. The most widespread of all is the prickly pear, which produces pink or orange pear- or egg-shaped fruits at the end of its paddles. Prickly pear cacti have been grown for thousands of years as a crop, and in some parts of Mexico, it remains as important to local people as maize! Prickly pear fruit are not just eaten, but also used to make delicious fruit drinks.

RECOMMENDED VARIETIES

The two most common species of dragon fruit differ mainly in the colour of their flesh. Both taste similar, but the fruits of *Hylocereus costaricensis* contain indicaxanthin, a deep reddish-purple pigment with antioxidant properties. Eating a lot of these can turn your pee and poo red for a while, which can be alarming but is nothing to worry about! Both species produce enormous, beautiful flowers that only open at night. In the wild, these are pollinated by nocturnal bats and moths.

HOW TO GROW

Despite its exotic appearance, dragon fruit is easy to grow, just so long as you keep it dry enough during really cold weather and protect it from temperatures below freezing. Ideally it should be kept above 10°C.

Dragon fruit do best in dry, subtropical climates, but can be grown in temperate areas, particularly in the far south of the UK or elsewhere in conservatories. Seeds can be sown in a free-draining potting mix such as that used for cactus. Germination generally takes one to four weeks in warm conditions, but occasionally longer. Growing from seed is easy, but it can take about two years for plants to start flowering, so if you know someone with a dragon fruit, it is a little faster to start from a cutting, but not quite so much fun.

Funky fruit & veg

HOW TO GROW

In the summer, the plants can be watered weekly, allowing the soil to almost dry out before watering again. This watering regime is fine so long as temperatures don't fall much below 18°C. In colder conditions, watering should be infrequent or withheld entirely. Mature dragon fruit plants will bear fruit throughout the warmer months, typically June to October. Try to keep your dragon fruit plant in the sunniest and warmest spot you can find and, while it is actively growing in the spring and summer, feed it regularly with a good organic fertiliser in pellet form. An adult dragon fruit plant will need a large pot about 30cm deep and 50cm or more in diameter. They have shallow roots, so the width of the pot is more important than its depth.

Dragon fruit plants can grow very large, so it is important to train them. Tie one or two main stems against a thick stake or other support, and then trim away any other side shoots – these can be used as cuttings to produce more plants. Once the stems have reached the height you choose (chest height is ideal), cut-off their growing tips. This might seem drastic, but it will encourage branching shoots to form at the top of the plant. These can then be allowed to spread outwards to hang downwards. Since flowers are only produced on new shoots, this is something you will need to repeat each year. Simply remove some of the longer shoots at the end of the flowering season to provide space for new growths to develop next season.

Each flower lasts only one night, and so unless you have plenty of moths swooping around your home, you will need to pollinate them after dark by transferring pollen from flower to flower with a soft paintbrush. The fruit will take about a month to ripen, depending on temperatures and sunlight. Look at the wing-like protrusions all over the fruit – these will be yellowish and starting to wither when the fruit is mature, while the fruit itself should feel ever so slightly squishy when you gently squeeze it. The skin cannot be eaten, but the flesh and seeds can be.

To produce new plants from cuttings, simply remove a segment 30–60cm long and allow it to dry for a week. This will allow the wounded end to seal up and prevent rotting. Thereafter, simply place the cut end into a pot of soil and keep the soil just moist, providing bright light but no direct sun until visible growth can be detected.

Dragon fruit | 119

Sensitive plants

Did you know that there are plants that have leaves that move as soon as you touch them and others that move on their own continually? A few plants have seed pods that explode and blast their seeds far away, and others have pods that squirt fluid to fly like a rocket!

Many plants have leaves that will turn to face the direction of the sun, or close up at night, or curl up or roll down in drought. But the sensitive plants are so called because their leaves or seed pods respond really quickly when touched!

Where do sensitive plants come from?

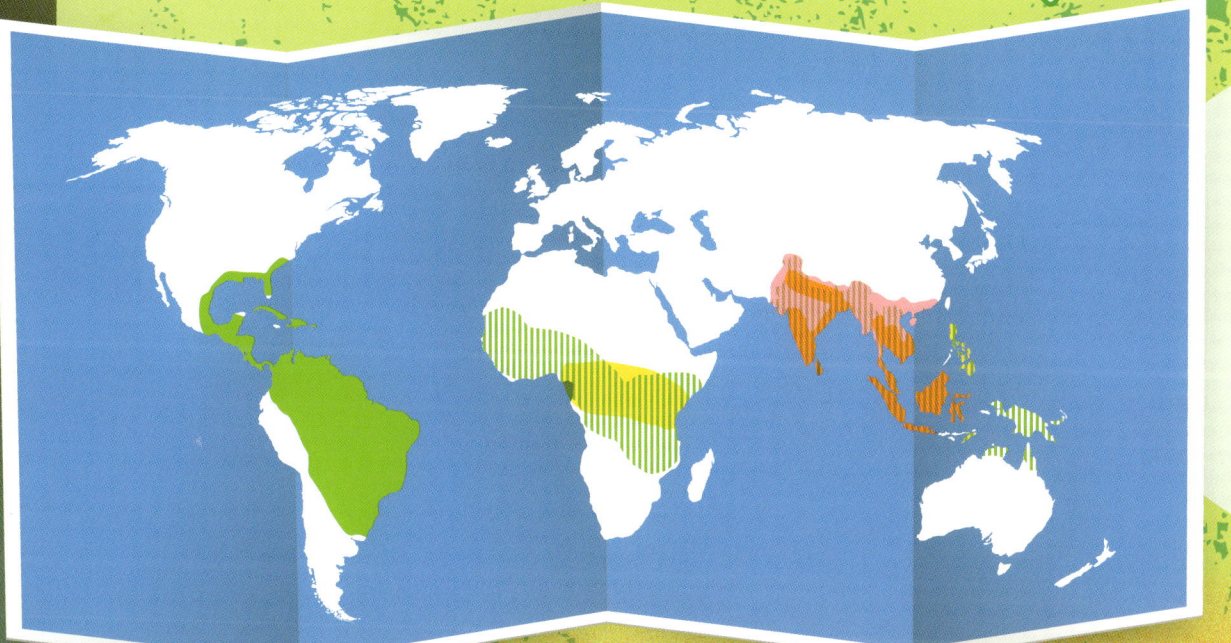

Sensitive plants are found across much of the world, although the most famous species (described in this chapter) are subtropical and tropical plants mainly from Asia.

- Codariocalyx
- Biophytum
- Mimosa native
- Mimosa invasive

WHY DO SENSITIVE PLANTS MOVE?

There are many reasons why plants have sensitive leaves. In a few cases, it is to capture and eat insects. The leaves of the famous Venus' Flytrap are sensitive and snap shut when tiny trigger hairs are touched. Sundews, butterworts and bladderworts also have deadly leaf traps that move, bend or curl when they capture prey to better kill and digest their victims (see Carnivorous Plants chapter, page 20).

Other sensitive plants, though, do not eat animals. Instead, they have leaves that fold up as a form of defence against leaf-eating insects or that move in order to bend towards the light to maximise photosynthesis.

The most common forms of rapid movement in the plant kingdom, though, are plants with explosive seed pods, which evolved to enable the plants to eject their seeds and spread widely.

121

EXPLODING SEED PODS

Hundreds of plant species have seed pods that explode to disperse their seed. Two of the most dramatic are:

WOOD SORRELS
(Oxalis)

Oxalis are a large group of plants found worldwide, with about 550 known species. While many of them are grown for their beautiful clover-like leaves alone, many species also produce very pretty flowers. And if that wasn't enough, the seed pods of many species explode once they ripen.

Oxalis stricta, the Yellow Wood Sorrel, is the best example of this, but many of the *Oxalis* sold by seed suppliers as ornamentals do exactly the same thing. *Oxalis tetraphylla* and *O. triangularis* are two alternative species that are very popular to grow, with especially beautiful leaves!

When ripe, the seed pods become very sensitive and, if touched, their sides dramatically split, flinging out seeds in all directions, as far as 3m away! The seeds pods of many ornamental *Impatiens*, an unrelated group of plants, also fling their seeds out dramatically over similar distances. You can almost guarantee that any plant nursery will have either ornamental *Impatiens* or *Oxalis* for you to try, and they thrive in identical conditions!

HOW TO GROW

WOOD SORREL CULTIVATION

The wood sorrel (*Oxalis*) group is a large one, including species that are easy to grow, and others that are challenging. Fortunately, most sorrels you are likely to encounter will grow happily in a small or medium-sized pot in standard potting mix.

These tough plants require damp soil at all times, with bright light or even direct sun, provided they are not allowed to dry out. Ornamental oxalis, especially hybrids, are selected because they are forgiving and strong growing, so these are usually a safe bet to start with. As you get more adventurous, there are some truly weird-looking sorrels from desert regions with fat stems like cacti and succulents (e.g. *Oxalis megalorrhiza*). These take a little more care, but are easy to grow in a protected spot like a conservatory.

122 Sensitive plants

SQUIRTING CUCUMBER
(Ecballium elaterium)

The Squirting Cucumber is a member of the gourd family and is native to Europe, northern Africa, and temperate areas of Asia. It produces a scrambling stem up to 1.5m long, with triangular leaves and small, bell-shaped flowers.

The plant gets its unusual name from the fact that, when pollinated, oval, bluish green, 4–5cm-long seed pods form. When mature the pods are filled with a jelly-like liquid under high pressure. Similar to the wood sorrels, when the seed pods are ripe, they become extremely sensitive to the touch.

The slightest movement causes the pods to detach from the stem, and the high-pressure liquid that they contain jets out from a hole, like fire blasting out from the bottom of a rocket. The seeds are thrown out as the pod explosively blasts forward.

Within a second, the seeds and the pod may be squirted as much as 7m from the original plant!

The little rocket seed pods of the Squirting Cucumber are so effective in dispersing the seeds that the plant's scientific name comes from the Greek 'ekballein,' meaning to 'throw out'!

The Squirting Cucumber is **poisonous** and should never be eaten!

SEED DISPERSAL

The more widely plants can disperse their seeds, the greater the chances that they have to keep control of the habitat in which they grow and colonise new areas. Sensitive plants with exploding seed pods ensure that their seed can be dispersed very effectively!

Exploding seed pods

SENSITIVE MIMOSA
(Mimosa pudica)

Also called the sensitive plant and shy plant, this is perhaps the most famous sensitive plant of all. Its scientific name *pudica* is Latin for 'shrinking' alluding to the reaction of its leaves.

Sensitive Mimosa is a creeping or scrambling plant that forms a woody stem up to 1.5m long. It has little prickles along its stem and branches.

HOW IT MOVES

The foliage of Sensitive Mimosa is carried on short branches. When touched, the leaflets rapidly fold together, normally within less than a second. If touched a second time, the branches quickly droop downwards, also within a second or so.

It is believed that the foliage of the plant responds in this way to deter leaf-eating insects, for as soon as they climb on the leaves, their meal folds up and disappears!

Contact with any object can cause the leaves to close. Usually, all of the leaves of Sensitive Mimosa close during a rain storm. After stimulation, the foliage reopens a few minutes or hours later. Generally, the more sunlight and healthier the plant, the faster the reaction time of the leaves! All the leaves close when it gets dark each evening and reopen in the morning light.

FLOWERS

In addition to sensitive leaves, Sensitive Mimosa has beautiful pink pom pom flowers!

Its natural home

This plant is native to subtropical and tropical parts of Central and South America, but it has spread widely across the tropics, and is found across much of Asia, Africa and the north of Australia. It is particularly common along roadsides in sunny or partly shaded areas.

OTHER SPECIES OF SENSITIVE MIMOSA

There are eight other species of sensitive *Mimosa*, although *Mimosa pudica* is the most common and has the fastest movement response. These other species include the large *Mimosa diplotricha* and *M. pigra*, which look like small trees!

Sensitive Mimosa

LITTLE TREE PLANT
(Biophytum sensitivum)

The Little Tree Plant is so called because it resembles a little palm tree and is sometimes used as a tree substitute in terrariums and miniature gardens. The foliage is arranged in a rosette from the top of a stem that may be up to about 20cm tall.

HOW IT MOVES

When the leaflets of the Little Tree Plant are touched, they fold downwards, although somewhat more slowly than those of the Sensitive Mimosa. The leaves may take up to three seconds to fold completely.

Similar to Sensitive Mimosa, the movement response is a means of defence against leaf-eating insects. The little leaflets usually open again within a few hours. In this species, too, the healthier the plant, the faster the movement response.

Its natural home

This species originates from wet, tropical parts of Nepal, India and several neighbouring Southeast Asian countries.

The Little Tree Plant usually grows in shady places.

FLOWERS

The Little Tree Plant produces pink or yellow trumpet-shaped flowers. If pollinated, the resulting seed pods have clever methods of dispersing their seeds (see right).

TRAMPOLINE SEED DISPERAL

The seed pods of the Little Tree Plant open quickly, and can ping out seeds as they do so. When open, they form a star-shaped trampoline that faces directly towards the sky. Falling raindrops splash on the surface of the trampoline, and bounce the little seeds from the pods onto soil nearby!

Little Tree Plant

Dancing Plant
(Codariocalyx motorius)

Have you ever heard of a plant that can dance? Well, believe it or not, there is a groovy tropical shrub that can! It has little leaflets that rotate continually in a dancing motion, but even more amazingly, the movement of this plant is stimulated and quickened when the foliage is touched, exposed to sunlight, warmth, vibrations and even loud sounds (including rock music!).

The Dancing Plant is a member of the pea family. Its name *motorius* is inspired by the plant's mobile leaf parts. This species grows upright on a narrow stem, and reaches heights of up to 1.5m.

rotating leaflets

HOW THEY MOVE

Each leaf of the Dancing Plant is borne on a narrow, hinged stem. Along the length of the stem, growing between the larger leaves, there are pairs of small, narrow leaflets. It is these leaflets that move rapidly.

Throughout the day, the small leaflets slowly rotate, taking about three minutes to complete a full circle. If you watch patiently, you will see the slow, continual movement, that gives the impression that the plant is dancing.

The movement of the leaflets speeds up in warmer temperatures and when exposed to sunlight. At night, all parts of the foliage droop downwards when the party is over, and the plant finally goes to sleep.

Sensitive plants

Their natural home

The Dancing Plant naturally originates form Asia, and prefers a sunny habitat in warm, lowland areas.

FLOWERS

The Dancing Plant produces small, purple flowers which have two large petals with white streaks along their centres.

It is thought that the movement of the leaflets is a way to increase exposure of the leaves to sunlight. The small moving leaflets sense and track the brightest sources of sunlight to enable the larger leaves to move on their hinges, and better angle themselves towards the brightest light source. As the angle of the sun changes during the day, the continual sensing movement of the little leaflets allows the plant to accurately reposition its larger, heavier leaves without wasting energy.

Another thought is that the rapid movements are intended to deter potential leaf-eating insects.

THE DANCING PLANT'S FAVOURITE MUSIC

Many botanists have reported that the Dancing Plant's movements speed up when exposed to loud sounds including music. However, most botanists seem unable to agree as to what the Dancing Plant's favourite beat is. Some say heavy metal, others say punk rock! Why don't you grow your own and find out what tunes you think work best to get this plant moving!

HOW TO GROW

Sensitive plants are great fun to grow and many species are popular for their curiosity value. The easiest sensitive plant to grow, and the one with the most dramatic movement response is the Sensitive Mimosa.

How to grow Sensitive Mimosa

Sensitive Mimosa germinates and grows quickly. It is best grown indoors as an annual and best started from seed. Seeds are inexpensive and widely available from seed suppliers across the world.

Soak the seeds in warm tap water for 24–48 hours before you plant them, as this will encourage them to sprout faster.

Sow the seeds in spring or early summer, planting three seeds to a small flowerpot (e.g. 7cm in diameter) filled with moist, well-drained soil. A mix of two parts loam, two parts peat moss, and one part sand or perlite works well, but Sensitive Mimosa is not that fussy.

Plant the seeds so they are just covered with soil (5mm is ideal), and gently press the surface of the soil down. It is a good idea to plant several pots of seeds, as many fail to germinate.

Place the pots in a greenhouse or terrarium, or cover each pot with glass or cling film, and place in a warm, sunny location. Ensure that the soil remains moist, but not soggy, and the seeds should germinate in approximately 7–14 days.

As the seedlings grow, make sure the soil remains moist. If more than one seedling germinated in the same pot, gently replant the smallest and weakest seedlings without disturbing the healthier one, so that you end up with one seedling per pot.

As your plants grow, place the pots in a warm, sunny location, such as a windowsill or greenhouse. Sensitive Mimosa loves to grow in full sun, but will also grow healthily in partial shade too. Seedlings and mature plants require temperatures of 18–21°C. For best results, dilute a balanced fertiliser to half the strength recommended on the label and apply to the soil once a week.

Remember, Sensitive Mimosas may not close their leaves if they do not receive enough sun or temperatures are too cold, so if yours is a bit sluggish, place it in a brighter and warmer location.

Sensitive Mimosa is not particularly prone to pests or diseases, but it may become infested with red spider mites, mealy bugs, or thrips. Spraying the plant with a direct stream of water can help remove the pests.

Growing other sensitive plants

The Little Tree Plant and the Dancing Plant can both be grown by following the same instructions as Sensitive Mimosa.

The Little Tree Plant requires slightly warmer and more humid conditions than the Sensitive Mimosa, so is best grown in a terrarium, or in a glass tank or large sweet jar on a windowsill.

How to grow 131

Unbelievable spectacular plants

Plants are amazing! They are the ultimate survivors, growing in some of the hottest and driest corners of the globe as well as some of the world's wettest and coldest regions. Plants can be found as high as 5,500m, at altitudes where few animals can survive. In such extreme habitats, a few plants even make greenhouses from their own leaf parts to shelter from the elements.

Plants include the most massive organisms on the planet, as well as the longest-lived ones, which can grow for thousands of years. The diversity of shapes, forms and survival strategies of plants is almost endless. In this chapter, we will explore some of the most spectacular plants of all!

Some like it hot...

...others are just so cool!

IRIDESCENT-LEAVED PLANTS

Most leaves are green because they contain chlorophyll, the chemical used in photosynthesis. A few dozen species of plants from tropical areas across South America, Africa and Asia produce leaves that sparkle electric blue like peacock feathers. This iridescent blue shine is not a pigment, but the optical effect of reflected light, like the rainbow colours that sparkle on a DVD.

Three of the most spectacular iridescent-leaved plants are the Peacock Fern (*Selaginella willdenovii*) from South East Asia, the Sapphire Fern (*Elaphoglossum wurdackii*) from Venezula and Columbia and a little-known species called *Stegolepis hitchcockii* from Venezuela. In all three of these plants, the upper surface of the foliage shines a brilliant blue colour that is visible only from certain angles. On Mount Neblina in the south of Venezuela, thousands of the *Stegolepis hitchcockii* plants grow together, causing the landscape to sparkle and flicker blue as the leaves move gently in the wind.

Although lots of theories have been put forward, botanists do not know for certain why plants have iridescent leaves. It is not merely just a way to attract pollinators, since the iridescent ferns do not flower and the iridescent *Stegolepis* species bloom every so often but produce glimmering leaves throughout the year.

It may be that the iridescent shine serves to protect the leaves by reflecting the higher levels of ultraviolet (blue) light which are found at higher elevations, where many of the iridescent-leaved plants grow.

Concentrated ultraviolet light is known to have a damaging effect on the chloroplasts of most plant species and the iridescent *Stegolepis* grow on mountain summits exposed to very strong sunlight. Perhaps by reflecting the blue component of sunlight, the iridescent plants have evolved a form of natural sun screen? However, this idea doesn't explain why the iridescent *Selaginella* and *Elaphoglossum* have their blue shine, as these plants grow in dense shade!

Unfortunately, when brought into cultivation, the brilliance of the shine of many iridescent plants is lost or greatly reduced, even if cultivated plants are grown in conditions that accurately reflect the natural environment of the wild.

HOW TO GROW

A few iridescent plants species (mainly *Selaginella willdenovii* and another Asian fern *Microsorum thailandicum*) are quite easy to grow, and they do retain their beautiful iridescent coloration in culture. These two species are increasingly being offered for sale by commercial plant retailers and can be grown at home. Both of these ferns need warm, humid conditions and dappled light.
They can be grown in a shady position in a greenhouse, in a terrarium on a windowsill or in a conservatory.
But remember if grown in either only direct sunlight or only dense shade, the iridescence will fail to form.

DARTH VADER BEGONIA

Begonias are a diverse group of plants that grow on the ground in rainforests in tropical areas across the world. Approximately 1,800 species are currently known, with many new ones continuing to be discovered and named. In 2014, a new Begonia was found in Sarawak on the island of Borneo. Its leaves are so intensely green that they almost appear black, and so it was named *Begonia darthvaderiana* after Darth Vader, from the Star Wars films.

This Darth Vader Begonia was found growing in deep shade below a forested cliff. The very dark coloration enables its leaves to absorb what little sunlight can pass through the dense layers of vegetation in the rainforest.

The botanists who named the Darth Vader Begonia also discovered a larger species of Begonia with silver and green leaves that they named *Begonia amidalae*, after another Star Wars character, Padmé Amidala, Luke Skywalker and Princess Leia's mother. Those Begonia botanists must have been serious Star Wars fans! If you discover a new species, you could name it after anything or anyone you like!

The Darth Vader Begonia is not easy to grow, but it is starting to become more widely available. It needs dark conditions, high humidity and warm temperatures. It can be grown successfully in terrariums, in warm greenhouses below benches, or in bathrooms, often on beds of moist volcanic stones to keep humidity high.

AMAZING AIRPLANTS

In the bromeliad family there is a group of about 650 species called airplants (*Tillandsia*) which are found in the Americas. Many airplant species are extremely common in parts of tropical South and Central America, and most grow as epiphytes, that is plants that grow on other plants, and festoon the branches of their host trees.

Airplants are so called because they, usually, do not need soil (see the information box opposite). Airplants come in many strange shapes and forms, often as balls of short, spiky leaves. Most species change colour when they flower and turn brilliant shades of bright red or pink to attract moths, hummingbirds and even bats, which act as pollinators!

A PLANT THAT DOESN'T NEED PLANTING!

Airplants get virtually all of the nutrients and water they need from their leaves. Their foliage is covered with little white, hair-like structures that increase their surface area to boost nutrient and water absorption from the air, rain, dew and any dust or dead leaves that fall on the plants. Therefore, the roots are only used to anchor the airplants onto the branch or tree trunk where they grow.

Unbelievable spectacular plants

HOW TO GROW

Airplants are easy and fun to grow. As they do not need soil, they can be grown almost anywhere, although growing them on bathroom windowsills, and in conservatories and shady greenhouses works particularly well. They have a few simple requirements.

Most airplants prefer bright, dappled light, rather than constant direct sunlight or continuous shade. Avoid dimly lit locations.

They need humidity and must be watered frequently, but also must be allowed to dry out between waterings, otherwise they rot and die. Often the easiest way is to spray them with a mister. Many growers find that a soaking mist once or twice a week in summer and once a month in cooler weather works well.

Most species prefer to grow in a temperature range of 10–32°C, and if possible, position them in a place where they get good air circulation.

Airplants grow well mounted to pieces of orchid bark, but are often sold attached to shells and decorative ceramic pieces. Mounting an airplant is really easy. The simplest way is to use a glue gun. The hot glue doesn't harm the airplant in any way, although never use super glue, which can be poisonous to airplants!

To encourage flowering, apply bromeliad fertiliser at half strength twice a month during the summer growing season. The flowers can last from several days to many months depending on the species. Each airplant dies after flowering, but several new offshoots (known as 'pups') typically emerge from the base of the airplant, and these will grow into new plants. If left, eventually a clump of airplants will form. Separate the pups and mount them separately if you wish to divide or propagate your airplant.

Amazing airplants 137

Beautiful Bromeliads

As well as airplants, the bromeliad family includes many other groups of interesting plants that grow on the branches of trees. Many bromeliads are called rainbow plants because they produce some of the most colourful leaves of all plants, especially when flowering.

There are about 3,500 species of bromeliads that grow across tropical and subtropical areas of the Americas, although there is just one species that also occurs in tropical West Africa.

The leaves of bromeliads usually grow in a rosette. In many species, the centre of the rosette forms a little pool (see information box). When flowering, the leaves may become bright shades of red, purple, yellow, gold, white or even blue!

Bromeliads range greatly in size. The smallest are only a few centimetres tall, while the biggest can be enormous (see the Giant Bromeliad (*Puya raimondii*) in the Unbelievable Flowers chapter, page 52. Most species are 20–45cm across. The Pineapple (*Ananas comosus*) is a bromeliad and the only one that is edible!

A PLANT WITH A POOL!

Growing on the branches of trees most bromeliads do not have roots, like those of most plants that grow into soil to absorb nutrients and water. They survive by collecting rainwater and dead leaves in their leaf rosettes. In many species (known as tank bromeliads), the leaves are arranged tightly to store a pool of water at the centre of the foliage that acts as the plant's water supply. Many animals, particularly frogs, live in the bromeliads' pools or use them to rear their young!

HOW TO GROW

Most bromeliads are tropical plants that love high levels of humidity and warm temperatures so your bathroom windowsill makes an excellent space for many bromeliad species. They may also be grown in conservatories and greenhouses, often in hanging baskets. Although some bromeliads will grow in dense shade, most prefer dappled light or bright conditions for at least a few hours of the day. However, a windowsill with direct sunlight all day long will scorch most bromeliads.

Many bromeliads have small root systems, so they can be kept in small pots and don't need to be repotted often. Many bromeliads do not need much water, especially those that have pools in their leaf rosettes, so don't sit them in a tray of water or their roots may rot. For best results, choose a pot or hanging basket with large drainage holes, and a potting mix that drains freely. Loose mixes of rich soil, perlite, vermiculite and orchid bark works well. Water your bromeliad when the soil is dry to the touch and ensure the 'pool' in the centre of the leaves is topped up with water.

You do not need to fertilise bromeliads, but to encourage flowering, you can apply a bromeliad fertiliser (available from large garden centres). Similar to airplants, most bromeliad plants will die after flowering, although several offshoots quickly develop and can be divided and planted separately or left to form a large, colourful clump.

Some of the most colourful and easiest bromeliads to grow are *Aechmea*, *Bilbergia*, *Dyckia*, *Guzmania* and *Vriesea*. Many of these will be available in your local garden centre.

Beautiful bromeliads

Spectacular Succulents

Succulents are plants that are adapted to growing in dry areas of the world by producing thick fleshy leaves and stems that store water. There are hundreds of unrelated groups of plants that botanists include together as succulent plants, and many are really colourful and interesting to grow at home.

Succulents come in all shapes, sizes and forms, but some of the most interesting are listed below.

The pebble plant (*Lithops*) comes from South Africa and Namibia, and grows underground except for two thick leaves that emerge above the level of the soil and are coloured to look just like pebbles! The plant is a master of disguise, and is both camouflaged from animals that might like to eat it, and protected under the soil from the extreme heat of the desert!

The window plant (*Fenestraria*) also comes from Namibia and also grows mostly underground, buried by sand, but this plant produces lots of thick leaves, each with a totally clear window on top. In the wild, the sun is very bright. Sunlight shines into the thick leaves through the clear windows, but the rest of the plant is safely protected underground, just like the pebble plant!

Unbelievable spectacular plants

Living jewel plants (*Titanopsis*) occur across southern Africa and grow above ground and have really tough leaves that resemble limestone. They are called living jewels because they produce beautiful yellow and white flowers.

Many species of *Crassula*, *Echeveria* and *Sempervivum* are widely grown succulents, and a lot of these produce compact, low-growing, colourful rosettes of thick, fleshy leaves, often with white or pearly bands and blotches.

The genus *Haworthia* is a group of about 150 varied species that grow in rosettes. A few species have transparent sections at the tips of their leaves and can function like the window plant even when covered in sand!

Aloes, *Euphorbia* and *Kalanchoe* are among the more popular upright-growing succulents, and many of these produce beautiful foliage with unusual forms and colours.

Spectacular succulents

How to Grow

Many succulents are extremely easy to grow, but most species cannot tolerate freezing temperatures, so are best grown on windowsills, in conservatories or heated greenhouses. Choose a location with bright light, but not strong direct sunlight. If your succulent plant is receiving too much sunlight, its leaves may turn white or yellowish.

Keep your succulent plant at a temperature of 21–32°C during the summer months, and 10–20°C during winter.

Choose a shallow pot or container that has drainage holes and use a cactus mix (available from garden centres) or make your own soil by mixing equal parts of potting compost, perlite or grit and sand. The soil you use must be gritty and free draining.

Water your succulent when the top of the soil has dried out. Never put it in a tray of standing water as this will cause the roots to rot. Overwatering is the biggest cause of failure with succulents (especially the pebble and window plants). Remember, succulents are extremely tolerant of drought and can survive months without rain. Never allow water to collect in a succulent's rosette as this will cause the plant to rot and die.

Succulents also rot if kept in humid or dimly lit areas, especially if they are overwatered. Apply a standard fertiliser once in spring and once in late autumn. Don't fertilise your plants in winter.

Many succulent plants naturally produce offsets, and these can be gently divided from the mother plant, potted up and treated as an adult.

Some species have thick, fleshy leaves that are easy to detach and can be used to make cuttings very simply. Gently detach the leaf and place it in a shady, dry area for three days to allow the cut surface of the cutting to seal and form a callus. Then lie the cuttings on top of a pot of succulent soil (rather than planting them, which makes them far more prone to rot). Within three months, roots should form. During the first summer season, water the cuttings once a week, then after this treat as adult succulent plants.

142 Unbelievable spectacular plants

COOL CACTI

Cacti are highly adapted to surviving in deserts, and unlike most plant species, grow as a stem without typical photosynthesising leaves. In many cacti, the stem itself is green and makes energy from sunlight. Many have stems that are pleated, allowing the cactus to rapidly expand as it absorbs water when rain does fall in these dry habitats.

There are over 1,750 species of cacti and all come from the Americas. Some are enormous, such as the massive Saguaro Cactus (*Carnegiea gigantea*) which stands 12m tall, can live for 150 years and can weigh 2,200kg! Others may be just a few centimetres tall.

Some cacti take the form of columns, others are spherical, and some consist of flat paddles. A few produce edible fruit, such as the prickly pear or the dragon fruit plant see page 116.

DANGEROUS SPINES!

In the dry areas where cacti grow, water is extremely valuable, and many animals would eat cactus plants if they could. Most cacti defend themselves by producing spines. The spines are actually highly modified leaves. In some species, they are tiny and break off, causing irritation in victims. In others, the spines are rigid and up to 20cm long!

A few species of cacti only produce spines when they are seedlings.

Cactus Flowers

Cacti generally grow in arid areas, where there are relatively few pollinators, so many of them produce large and brightly coloured flowers to attract the few pollinators that there are. The desert landscape can erupt in a rainbow of colours at certain times of the year when cacti bloom!

Unusual Cacti

For decades, horticulturists have grafted mutant strains of cacti (particularly *Gymnocalycium mihanovichii*) that lack chlorophyll (and so appear bright red, orange or yellow) onto another cactus plant. The resulting combined plant is called a 'Moon Cactus' and can be grown following precisely the same growing conditions as regular ungrafted cacti plants.

The Unicorn Horn Cactus (*Eulychnia castanea 'spiralis'*) has been bred to grow abnormally with a twisted stems and bizarre looking rows of spines. *Cereus forbesii 'spiralis'* is a similar, twisted, spiral cactus, shown right.

Unbelievable spectacular plants

HOW TO GROW

Many cacti are very easy to grow and can be cultivated in the same way as succulent plants (see the previous pages). Some species will produce flowers very frequently when grown on a windowsill or in a greenhouse or conservatory; others will never bloom when grown indoors.

As with succulent plants, you are more likely to kill cacti by overwatering them than underwatering. So if in doubt, keep your cactus dry.

Be extremely careful when repotting cacti, and wear thick gloves to protect yourself from the cactus plant's sharp spines!

Many cacti require very little care and can be left alone for weeks at a time, making them very easy to grow. It is fun to plant attractive displays of many species of cactus (and succulent plants) together in large, shallow pots or containers.

Cool cacti 145

ARMOURED PLANTS

Through photosynthesis, plants create energy in the form of sugars from carbon dioxide, water and sunlight. The creation of this energy fuels virtually all life on Earth, and almost all animals depend upon plants to survive (either by eating them, or eating animals that eat plants).

But plants have evolved many ways to defend themselves from the attacks of animals. Many plants have poisonous saps, while others have ferocious spines, sometimes backwards-pointing barbs that make the spines especially painful!

STINGING PLANTS

A few plants cover their leaves with needles that have chemicals that deliver a painful sting, such as the stinging nettle. In Australia, there are a group of plants called stinging trees. One species, *Dendrocnide moroides*, has perhaps the most powerful sting of all, its sting is so painful that it has been known to kill dogs, horses, and drive humans mad with agony.

Stringing trees are covered with tiny needles that are so fine they can't be removed with tweezers. Just brushing against the large, heart-shaped leaves causes the sting, which botanist Marina Hurley described as 'being burned by hot acid and electrocuted at the same time'!

Cyril Bromley, another victim of the stinging tree, had to be strapped to a hospital bed for three weeks because of the pain caused by falling into a patch of leaves.

Unbelievable spectacular plants

GREENHOUSE PLANTS

Plants often have very clever ways to survive in extreme conditions. Growing in the highlands of Tibet, at over 4,000m, two plants (*Rheum alexandrae* and *Saussurea medusa*) use their leaves in a novel way to create their own greenhouses. In *Rheum alexandrae*, large, expanded, cream-coloured leaves cover the flowers, protecting them from the wind and cold. In *Saussurea medusa*, the whole plant grows in a compact ball of foliage. Dense hairs develop between the leaves, and completely insulate the plant, creating an appearance a bit like a sea urchin! Through these adaptations, both species can live in landscapes of almost bare rock, where few other plants can survive.

1 RECORD HOLDERS

The world's biggest blooms are documented in the Unbelievable Flowers chapter (pages 48 to 53), but what are the other record holders of the plant world?

THE PLANT WITH THE BIGGEST SEED

The world's biggest seed is produced by the Coco de Mer (*Lodoicea maldivica*), a species of palm from the Seychelles Islands in the Indian Ocean.

Each seed is up to 50cm across, can weigh up to 42kg and can take seven years to mature! The scientific name is derived from Greek words meaning 'beautiful buttocks'!

The name Coco de Mer, french for sea coconut, also has an interesting story. French explorers found the giant seeds washed up on the coast of East Africa and islands in the Indian Ocean and for centuries, it was believed by many, that the seeds were produced by a mystical coconut palm that grew at the bottom of the ocean! Eventually, Coco de Mer plants were discovered growing on the islands of the Seychelles and in 1768 the myth was exploded.

THE PLANT WITH THE BIGGEST LEAF

There are many ways to categorise leaves, but the Raffia Palm (*Raphia farinifera*) of the Mascarene Islands has the largest leaves of any plant. They can reach 25m long by 3m wide, but are made up of around 180 separate leaflets.

The biggest undivided leaf of all is produced by the Elephant Ear Plant (*Alocasia robusta*) from Borneo (below). One was measured to be over 3m long and 2m wide, although there are reports of this species producing leaves over 4.5m long and 2.5m wide! Several giant-leaved *Anthurium* species may produce leaves near as large too, such as *Anthurium metalicum* and *A. salgarense*.

Although we usually think of plants as growing on land, kelp plants form massive underwater forests, and may produce leaves that are over 100m in length! So if we include underwater plants in this category, kelp are the true record holders!

THE WORLD'S TALLEST TREE

The tallest trees in the world are Coast Redwoods (*Sequoia sempervirens*), which tower above the ground in California and south-western Oregon. These gigantic trees typically grow to over 90m high. A particularly tall specimen, named Hyperion, was discovered in 2006 and measured 115.85m in 2009, making it the tallest tree alive on the planet!

Record holders

THE WORLD'S MOST MASSIVE TREE

The world's most massive tree (largest by volume) is the Giant Sequoia (*Sequoiadendron giganteum*) in California. The largest known tree is named General Sherman and is truly enormous. It has been estimated to be over 1,487 cubic meters in volume, about 2,000 years old and 83m tall.

Although General Sherman is the most massive tree alive today, it is not the biggest ever recorded. That record goes to a coast redwood cut down in 1940 which was believed to have been over 1,800m^3 in volume, and an even bigger one (estimated at 2,500m^3) was reported in a 1905 newspaper article!

Thousands of these massive, ancient trees were cut down for timber over the last 200 years, but fortunately, the commercial felling of redwoods and sequoias has stopped.

Unbelievable spectacular plants

OLDEST PLANT ON EARTH

Many plants can live for thousands of years, but California's Bristlecone Pines (*Pinus longaeva*) have the longest lives of all organisms on Earth. This species has hardly changed for hundreds of millions of years, as can be seen in fossils which are almost identical to the living trees. The oldest Bristlecone Pine known to scientists grows in California's White Mountains, and is believed to be 5,068 years old.

Just imagine, this same tree was alive and growing when the pyramids in Egypt were being built!

Record holders 151

OTHER TIME TRAVELLERS

Bristlecone Pines may be the oldest living organisms on Earth, but many other plant species have extremely long lives.

Baobab trees live in dry areas of southern Africa, Madagascar and Australia. They are known as bottle trees because the are shaped like a bottle, with large, swollen trunks. Inside, they have spongy wood so that when it rains, they absorb (often tonnes) of water really quickly, and can then store it for months or even years in the trunk. Some boababs are really wide. One tree in South Africa named locally as Glencoe Baobab (*Adansonia digitata*) has a circumference of 47m and a diameter of over 15m! Baobabs can live for over 2,000 years, and the oldest one known (a tree from Zimbabwe) was estimated to be 2,450 years old when it died in 2011.

152 Unbelievable spectacular plants

Another incredible 'time traveller' plant grows in the deserts of Namibia and Angola – some of the driest places on Earth. It is called *Welwitschia mirabilis*. The word *mirabilis* means 'miracle' in Latin, and this plant really is miraculous. Like the Bristlecone Pine, it is often called a 'living fossil' as it has remained unchanged for millions of years. *Welwitschia* is a really peculiar plant. It is related to pine trees and produces cones, although the plant itself looks nothing like a conifer.

Welwitschia only ever produces two adult leaves! They grow continuously (the leaves die at their tips, but grow at their bases, so always stay around the same length). Each leaf grows by around 1cm a year, and many plants have leaves that have living sections of 2m or longer (before the end of the leaf dies and breaks apart). So the tips of these very leaves were produced up to 200 years ago, before Charles Darwin was alive! But the really amazing fact about Welwitschia is that each plant can live for over 2,000 years (some scientists say much longer).

Record holders 153

AMAZING BONSAIS

For over 2,000 years, Japanese, Chinese and Korean horticulturists have perfected the art form of growing bonsais to produce miniature trees that mimic the shape and scale of full-grown trees. This is accomplished by continually clipping the roots and branches of the bonsai to ensure its growth is stunted, so that the tree can never reach its natural, full size.

Particularly in Japan, some bonsais have been grown by the same family for centuries, and are passed down between the generations. Several bonsai trees are known to be over 700 years old, and a few have existed for over 1,000 years! Large bonsais need care virtually every day, so somebody must have attended to these ancient trees constantly since the year 1000. Imagine growing a pot plant and giving it to your children in the hope that in a thousand years' time, the ancestors of your children will be still growing the very same plant!

Possibly the most incredible bonsai of all is a Japanese White Pine. At 390 years old, it is quite young for a bonsai, but what makes it amazing is that it was growing in Hiroshima when the first atomic bomb was dropped in 1945. 160,000 people died in the devastating Hiroshima blast, but remarkably, it survived and is still growing today in the U.S. National Arboretum. A gift from the family who had cared for it for five generations as a symbol of friendship and connection.

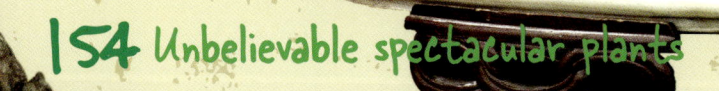

154 Unbelievable spectacular plants

HOW TO GROW

Bonsais are fun to grow, and you don't have to wait hundreds of years to see great results. Although you can grow your bonsai from tree seeds, it may take several years for the seeds to grow to a size to start with, so generally, it is best to buy a starter tree (a small tree ready to be shaped as a bonsai).

The secret of growing bonsai lies in planting your tree in a shallow pot (so the roots are restricted), trimming the roots and leaves frequently (so the tree remains stunted), and shaping the growth of the branches and foliage by using wire to force the tree to grow in a particular shape, and selectively trimming branches and leaves to keep that growth form.

Growing conditions for bonsais vary depending upon which species of tree is used. Temperature, watering and soil must all match the needs of the bonsai species' natural requirement. Bonsais created using temperate tree species may be grown outside all year round, whereas bonsais of subtropical or tropical tree species will need to be kept inside a conservatory or greenhouse.

Visit your local garden centre and choose a starter tree to suit the conditions you can provide, then pot your starter tree in a shallow container, and start shaping your very own bonsai tree!

Amazing bonsais

Sourcing spectacular plants

If you are hunting for good places to locate plants and seeds, there are a number of different options open to you.

For beginners, dedicated plant societies will often provide guides and websites offering huge amounts of information about how to grow your plants, and in many cases they also maintain plant and seed sales lists.

Reputable nurseries can offer excellent advice, whether you turn up in person or call them on the phone, while seed sellers will often provide general instructions on their seed packets.

RHS Plant Finder

www.rhs.org.uk/plants/search-form

The above website offers a unique tool that enables users to search for suppliers of plants via a database compiled from the catalogues of a vast array of commercial plant sellers.

Not only does this provide a great resource to locate rare or difficult-to-find plants, but refine tools allow the user to process search results by preferences, such as size, hardiness, colour etc., to identify the most suitable plant species.

Where are the best places to buy plants?

RHS Plants – www.rhsplants.co.uk
The Royal Horticultural Society's online nursery.

RHS Garden Wisley – www.rhs.org.uk/gardens/wisley
RHS Garden Wisley operates a well-stocked nursery of many RHS-awarded plants for visitors.

Rareplants Nursery – www.rareplants.co.uk
A nursery offering one of the widest selections of rare and unusual species, particularly bulbs and tubers, including many hardy orchids. The catalogue is seasonal and is published twice a year.

Tropical Britain Nursery – www.tropicalbritain.co.uk
Specialising in exotic plants, particularly exotics that can survive the British climate.

Crûg Farm Plants – www.crug-farm.co.uk
Offering a wide range of rare and unusual hardy plants not seen elsewhere.

Organic Plants – www.organicplants.co.uk
Specialising in vegetables and fruits, both plants and seeds.

Thompson and Morgan – www.thompson-morgan.com
One of the largest sellers of plant seeds, including flowers, fruits, vegetables, ornamentals, grasses and trees.

Fruit moulds

www.fruitmould.com
Suppliers of fruit and vegetable moulds.

Plant societies

Royal Horticultural Society – www.rhs.org.uk
Perhaps the world's most recognised and respected gardening society with extensive libraries of advice, pictorial guides, and regular shows.

Carnivorous Plant Society – www.thecps.org.uk
Specialising in carnivorous plants of all kinds, with an excellent seed list.

European Palm Society – www.palmsociety.org.uk
Palm specialists, offering an exhaustive list of palm suppliers worldwide.

International Asclepiad Society (for starfish flowers) – www.asclepiadinternational.org
Offering cultivation instructions, sources of plants and an academic newsletter.

Garden Organic – www.gardenorganic.org.uk
Specialising in fruits and vegetables, including a heirloom seed list of classic kitchen plants.

Alpine Plant Society – www.alpinegardensociety.net
Specialising in small woodland plants, hardy plants, climbers, bulbs and shrubs, with a seed list of over 5,000 species.

Hardy Plant Society – www.hardy-plant.org.uk
Offering a seed list of over 2,000 tempting varieties of rare, unusual and familiar seeds.

International Aroid Society (for arums and more) – www.aroid.org
Offering a newsletter, cultivation and pollination guides, as well as a trading post.

Photographic credits

The publisher and author would like to thank all those photographers and image makers who have contributed to this book. All photographs are credited to the author Stewart McPherson except those credited below. All illustrations are credited to Marc Dando except those credited below.

Key: t = top; tl = top left; tr = top right; tc = top centre; c = centre; b = bottom; bl = bottom left; br = bottom right. IS = iStock; SS = Shutterstock.

Half title and backgrounds throughout mamanamsai/SS; **2** joloei/SS; **5** rattiya lamrod /SS; **6** Michelle Holihan /SS; **7** bl Igor Tichonow /SS; **8** br juerginho /SS; **9** tl Yes Daddy/SS, bl krasky/SS, tr Emily Li/SS, cr boyphare/SS, br Natalya Osipova/SS; **11** bl Kinoya /SS; **12** Gerardo C.Lerner/SS; **13** Dr Morley Read/SS; **14 & 15** Janos Levente/SS; **16** bl Eva Kali/SS, bl Bildagentur Zoonar GmbH/SS, tr Stefano Garau/SS, br Julia Shepeleva/SS; **17** tl Oprea George/SS, bl Jon Manjeot/SS, tr diy13/SS, br Mihashi/SS; **18** tr Chim/SS, br Vaclav Volrab/SS; **19** r Prachaya Roekdeethaweesab/SS; **20** l Marco Uliana/SS, r Cathy Keifer/SS; **21** l Cathy Keifer/SS; **22** br Andrew Fleischmann/SS; **23** bl Aggie 11/SS; **24** bl Noah Elhardt/CC BY-SA 2.5; **25** tl Marco Maggesi/SS, bl Henri Koskinen/SS, br Stéphane Joly; **27** tl Linas T/SS, bl Jojoo64/SS, box tr Martin Fowler/SS, box ml Olexandr Taranukhin/SS; **28** l EQRoy/SS, tr Barry Rice, br Luka Hercigonja/SS; **29** bl Barry Rice, bl Jeff Holcombe/SS, box br PeingjaiChiangmai/SS; **30** l Stephen Fretwell; **31** tl Kelly Marken/SS, box tl Horst Lieber/SS, box tc Nokuro/SS, box tr Chun photographer/SS, box bl Serguei Koultchitskii/SS, box bc Mr.Lersom Loungpon/SS, box br Mercury Green/SS; **32** l Jean Faucett/SS; **33** tl Gstrau/SS, bl Hanjo Hellmann/SS, tr ordinary man/SS, br Jeff McGraw/SS; **38** l Kitty Bern/SS, r Chris Moody/SS; **39** tl Marty Pitcairn/SS, bl Mat Millar, tr goodgold99/SS, br Guillermo Guerao Serra/SS; **40** pikky/SS; **41** tl Grazyna Palaszewska/SS, cr Tropicalvision/SS; **42** tl Barry Rice, bl bebebyul/SS; **43** tl Gary Wheeler, cl Luis Carocci, bl Dylan Sheng, r Natalia Ramirez Roman/SS; **44** bl Suekarsa Suchai/SS, cr Gilbert S. Grant/SS; **45** bl Andy Smith/SS; **46** GaryP/SS; **47** l Dirk van der Walt/SS; **48** r Alexander Mazurkevich/SS; **49** WITTAYA BR/SS; **50** Isabelle OHara/SS; **51** l Brad Wilson, r Paul Marcus/SS; **52** l Christian Vinces/SS, r TravelStrategy/SS; **53** l Christian Vinces/SS, r tony mills/SS; **54** l cotosa/SS, r A.S.Floro/SS; **55** l Beatrice Sirinuntananon/SS, c songsak/SS, tr Mark Heighes/SS, br www.strangewonderfulthings.com; **56** tl Yukiakari/SS, bl Stephen Fretwell, r Jody./SS; **57** c Emilio100/SS, r www.strangewonderfulthings.com; **58** l Leela Mei/SS, r Gyro/IS; **59** l & bl www.flickr.com/photos/laajala/, r Wathana/SS; **60** tl Bos11/SS, bl Angel DiBilio/SS, c New Line/SS, r Stefan Scherer-Emunds/SS; **61** tl Flower_Garden/SS, bl pisitpong2017/SS, c Art65395/SS, r mspoli/SS; **62** tl atabik yusuf djufni/SS, r Han-Lin/SS; **63** l Kittisak Chysree/SS, tr electra/SS, br Dancestrokes/SS; **64** tl electra/SS, tc S-JO'/SS, r Philip Marsden/SS; **65** bl Soulikone Thongsamouth/SS, c honeymonster/SS, r Trevor Fairbank/SS; **66** l Yongkiet Jitwattanatam/SS, tc Don Mammoser/SS, tr Manfred Ruckszio/SS, cc NcCoTi/SS, cr alybaba/SS, b Sana Rahim/SS; **66 & 67** t PradaBrown/SS, c PROVENZA/SS; **67** tl p_nam/SS, cl Iulia Starova/SS, tc riet bloemen/SS, cc Del Boy/SS, bc & br Ludmila Ivashchenko/SS; **69** l Svetlana Larina/SS, cr kc_film/SS, br Ultraviolet_Photographer/SS; **70** l Ron Leishman/SS, r Albert Visage/FLPA; **71** l jaimie tuchman/SS, r F_studio/SS; **72** tl Ron Leishman/SS, t Crazy nook/SS; **73** l michel arnault/SS, r SLAVIANIN/SS; **74** l & r Djohan Shahrin/SS; **75** l nine_far/SS, r Bannafarsai_Stock/SS; **76** l Zvone/SS, r Man-Zu/SS; **77** l Nikolay Kurzenko/SS, r Kate Higgs/SS; **78** l Igor Batenev/SS, tr Pavaphon Supanantananont/SS, br Jiri Prochazka/SS; **79** tl Jane Bettany/SS, bl Jason Garnier/SS, r Amy CNLB/SS; **80** tr R.Yuta/SS, cr Piboon Suwankosai/SS, br Darko Pejcic/SS; **81** br Vastram/SS; **82** l Madelein Wolfaardt/SS, r Luka Hercigonja/SS; **83** tl nutriaaa/SS, bl InfoFlowersPlants/SS, r Gestiafoto/SS; **84** l R. Maximiliane/SS, r Milena Lachowicz/SS; **85** l David Fowler/SS, r Gary K Smith/FLPA; **86** l PRILL/SS; **87** l biosteam/SS, r Amawasri Pakdara/SS; **88** t jipatafoto89/SS, b Boonchuay1970/SS; **89** tc morethan123/SS, cc Hanjo Hellmann/SS, r Noppharat4969/SS; **90** l suriya9999/SS; **91** l Paul Fauntleroy, r Manfred Ruckszio/SS; **92** tl Neizu/SS, c CC BY 3.0/Amada44; r Flystock/SS; **93** l DutchMen/SS, r Hardy Plant Society; **94** tl Anna Kucherova/SS, tc Serenetho/SS, bl FPWing/SS, br Thumbelina/SS; **94 & 95** t Cynthia Liang/SS; **95** l Stephen Smith, r margouillat photo/SS; **96** l photogal/SS, r Michaelpuche/SS; **97** tl CG_Photography/SS, tcl ArtCookStudio/SS, cl Natalia Korshunova/SS, cbl Izlan Somai/SS, bl Alex Coan; **98** r D. Pimborough/SS; **99** l Irina Solatges/SS, r Marcel Jancovic; **100** l & tr 5PH/SS, tcr Rosemarie Mosteller/SS, bcr Viktor Lugovskoy/SS, br MPH Photos/SS; **101** r Amy Johansson/SS; **102** tl yuda chen/SS, c Kazakov Maksim/SS, r Y Photo Studio/SS; **103** l VectoryFloor/SS, tr Assabi najoua/SS, br Natasha Breen/SS; **104** tl Teri Virbickis/SS, cl id-art/SS, bl Dani Vincek/SS, tr neil langan/SS, cr CrackerClips Stock Media/SS, br c sa bum/SS; **105** S-F/SS; **106** tl & tr lineartestpilot /SS, b naramit/SS, cr LENA GABRILOVICH/SS; **107** l Lebedeva Olga/SS, r Ramon L. Farinos/SS; **108** tl Ramon L. Farinos/SS, cl picturepartners/SS, bl CC BY-SA 4.0/Didier Descouens, tr ThomasLENNE/SS, cr Halfmine.mamie/SS, br Neale Couslan/SS; **109** Marcus Padoongwong/SS; **110** cl Radoslav Kellner/SS, b Sarah Marchant/SS, tl Anjo Kan; **111** tr Anjo Kan/SS, br Kazakov Maksim/SS; **112** tl nikiteev_konstantin /SS, bl nutua/SS, tr CC2 Laughlin Elkin/SS; **113** box t & b fruitmould.com, bl Rashevskyi Viacheslav/SS, tr Sebastian Kaulitzki/SS, br fruitmould.com; **114** l Deenida/SS, r PathomP/SS; **115** l Paleka/SS, all r fruitmould.com; **116** tl Nipatsara Bureepia/SS, tc Sunwand24/SS, tr SOMCHAI DISSALUNG/SS; **117** tl darjalvova/SS, b DMHai, r Maria Uspenskaya/SS; **118** tl Boonchuay1970/SS, bl Pairoj Sroyngern/SS, r Uma_Der2/SS; **119** tl haireena/SS, br DD Images/SS; **120** Noppharat4969/SS; **121** br senengmotret/SS; **122** tl & tr wk1003mike/SS, c yxowert/SS; **123** l ChWeiss/SS; **124** l Doikanoy/SS; tr & tc AjayTvm/SS, br sutham/SS; **125** l Noppharat4969/SS, box pisitpong2017/SS, r sevenke/SS; **126** l wasanajai/SS, r AJI B/SS; **127** tl pisitpong2017/SS, b & r wasanajai/SS; **128** l CC BY-SA 3.0/Ks.mini; **129** l & r CC BY-SA 3.0/Ks.mini; **130** tl Assanai Srasoongnern/SS, bl Grisha Bruev/SS, br Fotocute/SS; **131** l Amihays/SS, r wasanajai/SS; **132** l Holli/SS, r LianeM/SS; **135** Avery Chan; **136** l Teerachai_P/SS, bl Sanit Fuangnakhon/SS, bc areeya_ann/SS, box NA HNWD/ss, r Ricardo de Paula Ferreira/SS; **137** b SOMKIET POOMSIRIPAIBOON/SS, tr Torsak Thammachote; **138** isarescheewin/SS, tl arxichtu4ki/SS, bl EQRoy/SS, bc Charles HB Mercer/SS, br Chayut Thanaponchoochoung/SS, tr sarayuth3390/SS; **139** box SUPEE PURATO/SS, bl marktucan/SS, br Steve Bower/SS; **140 & 141** asharkyu/SS; **140** tl & tr Irina Vaneeva/SS, cl Real Moment/SS, cc Eva Pieroni/SS, cr Vangelis_Vassalakis/SS; **141** bl ZEEN KAWEE/SS, tr Geert Naessens/SS, br mizy/SS; **142** tl anusart khotpet/SS, br Christina Siow/SS; **143** l StockPhotoAstur/SS, c elnavegante/SS, bc Celig/SS, r cpaulfell/SS, br Venus Kaewyoo/SS; **144** tl Konstantin Zaykov/SS, bl paisalphoto/SS, tr Sergey Granev/SS, cr Sarah2/SS; **145** bl prawin99/SS, tl MakroBetz/SS, br panattar/SS; **146** l krolya25/SS, bl Chrispo/SS, br Victoria Tucholka/SS; **147** l Yakov Oskanov/SS, tl pikepicture/SS, r Oleg Znamenskiy/SS; **149** l Irainy/SS, bl Dario Lo Presti/SS, r Lucky-photographer/SS, br Sundry Photography/SS; **150** l Simon Dannhauer/SS, br The Perfect/SS; **151** bl Oliclimb/SS, r Bill45/SS; **152** l Karel Gallas/SS, c GUDKOV ANDREY/SS; **152 & 153** Bruce Rolff/SS; **153** l Fabian Plock/SS, br Trek Bears Photography/SS; **154** tl & tr AKARIN CHATARIYAWICH/SS, tl TB studio /SS, br Jack.Q/SS; **155** bl Ketta/SS, tr GAMARUBA/SS, br GrooTrai/SS; **157** Halel2uya/SS; **158, 159, 160** backgrounds Val_Iva/SS.

Cover front tl Cherdchai Chaivimol/SS, bl vanchai /SS, br kamnuan/SS, background mamanamsai/SS; **back** l ThomasLENNE/SS, r Jody./SS.

About the author

Stewart McPherson is a British naturalist, author and film-maker. Fascinated by wildlife from an early age, he began writing his first book at the age of sixteen. Stewart went on to study geography at the University of Durham. On graduating, he spent ten years climbing 300 mountains across the world (some of which were previously unexplored), to study and photograph carnivorous plants in the wild. Along the way, he co-discovered and co-named 35 new species/varieties of carnivorous plants, including some of the largest pitcher plants ever discovered and wrote a series of 25 books.

After featuring in short sequences in several broadcast documentaries, Stewart and a camera team travelled to all of the UK Overseas Territories to document the wildlife, cultures, history and landscapes that the territories harbour. This journey took three years to complete, and the resulting documentary series was released as *Britain's Treasure Islands* on the BBC, National Geographic, SBS and many other channels. The accompanying *Britain's Treasure Islands* book was distributed across the UK, and (through sponsorship) were donated to 5,350 secondary schools and 2,000 libraries.

Stewart wrote this Spectacular Plants book and made 16 accompanying online films to inspire the passion of the next generation in horticulture, gardening and botany in general. He remains extremely grateful to the Don Hanson Charitable Foundation for sponsoring the donation of one copy of this work to each of 10,000 primary schools across the UK.

Amazing Pets

If you have enjoyed this book and would like to get more involved with nature, we have this accompanying title just for you. For more about this title visit our website at

www.wildnaturepress.com

Spectacular plant films online

Visit www.spectacularplants.com to see 14 videos made by Stewart McPherson exploring the world's most incredible plant species and how to grow them. Hundreds of photographs, key growing advice and further resources are also available at this website.

How to Grow Index

Aechmea species 139
airplants 137
Albany Pitcher Plant 45
aloes 142
Amorphophallus bulbifer 91
Amorphophallus konjac 91
Amorphophallus paeoniifolius 91
Amorphophallus species 91
Amorphophallus titanum 91
Antirrhinum majus 57
Aristolochia cymbifera 59
Aristolochia fimbriata 59
Aristolochia salvadorensis 59
Aristolochia tiracambu 59
bat flowers 63
Bilbergia species 139
Biophytum sensitivum 131
Bird of Paradise 65
Black tomatoes
   'Black Beauty' 100
   'Black Brandywine' 100
   'Black Cherry' 100
   'Black Krim' 100
   'Black Prince' 100
   'Cherokee' 100
   'Gigantomo' 100
bladderworts 43
Blue Passion Flower 67
bonsais 155
bromeliads 139
butterworts 42
cacti 145
carnivorous plants 40
carrots
   'Atomic Red' 97
   'Belgium White' 97
   'Cosmic Purple' 97
   'Purple Dragon' 97
   'Purple Haze' 97
   'Red Samurai' 97

   'Solar Yellow' 97
   'White Satin' 97
   'Yellowstone' 97
Cephalotus follicularis 45
Chiranthodendron pentadactylon 57
Codariocalyx motorius 131
Crassula species 142
cucamelons 111
Dancing Plant 131
Devil's Hand 57
Devil's Tongue 91
Dionaea muscipula 43
Dracula simia 57
Dracula vampira 59
Dracunculus vulgaris 85
dragon fruit 118
Dragon Lily 85
Drosera aliciae 41
Drosera capensis 41
Drosera regia 41
Drosera roraimae 41
Drosera slackii 41
Drosera spatulata 41
Dyckia species 139
Ecballium elaterium 131
Echeveria species 142
Euphorbia species 142
Fenestraria species 142
Four O'Clock Flower 61
giant arums 91
Guzmania species 139
Haworthia species 142
Heliamphora heterodoxa 45
Heliamphora nutan 45
Heliconia species 65
Hot Lips Flower 60
Hylocereus costaricensis 118
Hylocereus undatus 118
Impatiens bequaertii 57
iridescent plants 134

Kalanchoe species 142
Lithops species 142
Little Tree Plant 131
living jewel plants 142
lobster claw flowers 65
marsh pitcher plants 45
Microsorum thailandicum 134
Mimosa pudica 130
Mirabilis jalapa 61
Monkey Face Orchid 57
Nepenthes maxima 44
Nepenthes rafflesiana 44
Nepenthes ventricosa 44
North American pitcher plants 44
Oxalis megalorrhiza 122
Oxalis species 122
Passiflora caerulea 67
pebble plant 142
pineberries
   'Natural Albino' 99
   'White Carolina' 99
   'White D' 99
Pinguicula cv 'Weser' 42
Pinguicula esseriana 42
Pinguicula gigantea 42
Pinguicula moranensis 42
Pinguicula primuliflora 42
Pinguicula x kewensis 42
potatoes
   'Austrian Crescent' 104
   'Cranberry Red' 104
   'Duke of York' 104
   'Kerr's Pink' 104
   'Red Rose' 104
   'Russian Banana' 104
   'Yukon Gold' 104
Psychotria elata 60
Purple potatoes
   'Adirondack Blue' 104
   'Dragon Egg' 104

   'Purple Majesty' 104
   'Purple Pelisse' 104
   'Sapphire' 104
   'Shetland Black' 104
Sarracenia flava 44
Sarracenia leucophylla 44
Sarracenia purpurea 44
Selaginella willdenovii 134
Sempervivum species 142
Sensitive Mimosa 130
snapdragons 57
Squirting Cucumber 131
Stapelia variegata 80
starfish flowers 80
Strelizia reginae 65
succulents 142
sundews 41
sweetcorn
   'Black Aztec' 108
   'Bloody Butcher' 108
   'Glass Gem' 108
   'Oaxacan Green Dent' 108
   'Strawberry' 108
Tacca species 63
Tillandsia species 137
Titanopsis species 142
tropical pitcher plants 44
Typhonium venosum 93
Utricularia gibba 43
Utricularia livida 43
Utricularia sandersonii 43
Venus' Flytrap 43
Voodoo Lily 93
Vriesea species 139
watermelons, super-shaped 114
window plant 142
wood sorrel 122